The Secret Transcript of the Council of Bishops

The Secret Transcript of the Council of Bishops

A Dialogue on Homosexuality and Church Unity

Darren R. Cushman Wood

RESOURCE *Publications* • Eugene, Oregon

THE SECRET TRANSCRIPT OF THE COUNCIL OF BISHOPS
A Dialogue on Homosexuality and Church Unity

Copyright © 2015 Darren R. Cushman Wood. All rights reserved. Except for brief quotations in critical publications or reviews, no part of this book may be reproduced in any manner without prior written permission from the publisher. Write: Permissions, Wipf and Stock Publishers, 199 W. 8th Ave., Suite 3, Eugene, OR 97401.

Resource Publications
An Imprint of Wipf and Stock Publishers
199 W. 8th Ave., Suite 3
Eugene, OR 97401

www.wipfandstock.com

ISBN 13: 978-1-4982-3028-5

New Revised Standard Version Bible, copyright 1989, Division of Christian Education of the National Council of the Churches of Christ in the United States of America. Used by permission. All rights reserved.

Manufactured in the U.S.A.

In memory of my grandparents
Lloyd and Marian Covey
and in appreciation for the Cowbell Theologians

Contents

Acknowledgments | *ix*
Introduction | *xi*

Setting & Cast of Characters | 1
Part One | 3
Part Two | 41

Bibliography | 69

Acknowledgments

I WOULD LIKE TO thank the Center of Theological Inquiry for allowing me to participate in the Pastor-Theologian Program from which this project originated. After the program ended, part of our cohort group continued to meet, and for over ten years have enjoyed good conversations about ministry and theology. This group of "Cowbell Theologians" have tolerated, challenged, supported, and affirmed me. I am grateful to be a part of them.

I would also like to thank my friend and colleague Rev. Dr. Andrew Kinsey. A few years ago we engaged in a lengthy and heated conversation about the issues of homosexuality and doctrine through a series of emails. Those conversations are reflected in this book. Andy has been a holy friend who has challenged my thinking and supported my spirit.

I am grateful for the appointments I have served: Greensboro, Sugar Grove, East Tenth Street, Speedway, and North United Methodist Churches. Thank you to my home church, Bartlett Chapel United Methodist, and to my college congregation, Fairlawn United Methodist, for laying the foundation of my faith and ministry. Having traversed the spectrum of United Methodism, I am grateful for the insights I have gained from each of them. They have been a means of grace for me and my family.

Special thanks goes to Beth DeHoff for her assistance with the manuscript. Finally, a word of thanks to my wife Ginny and her patience with me.

Introduction

WHAT WOULD WESLEY SAY? United Methodists have always looked to their founder for an example or a quick quote to justify their actions. This dialogue is a little theological exercise to see what insights we might discover in the writings and practices of John Wesley in light of the ongoing debate over homosexuality and its impact on church unity.

Homosexuality raises a host of related questions and issues about ecclesiology. It serves as a good case study to explore how we understand the nature and mission of the church, the meaning of membership, and the role of the episcopacy. Wesleyans have never professed to have an explicit or even coherent understanding of the nature of the church. However, by putting Wesley in the midst of our conversation we may see a better way to understand the church and more loving way to move forward.

This originated as a project for the Pastor-Theologian Program of the Center of Theological Inquiry in 2006. It is also a reflection on my experiences as a delegate to two General Conferences. Over time it became an exercise in listening to the various voices in this debate and their underlying assumptions. It is my hope that there are no straw men in this dialogue but that the complexity of each opinion is honored. Nor is it my intention to align Wesley with a particular side of the debate. Rather, my goal is to listen to the tradition of Wesley in our contemporary context and to put him in conversation with us. We must let the tradition judge us and guide us.

Introduction

Why write a dialogue? For two reasons. One, the early Methodists did theology in conversation. The first annual conference was a conversation (with John, no doubt, dominating the debate) that expressed their theology in a question-and-answer form that was preserved and passed on in the minutes. This model of theological reflection can still serve us well. Two, the complexity of the issue and the diversity of perspectives warrants this form. A dialogue is the best way to capture the warp and woof of this forty year debate.

To be sure, this is fiction and any resemblance to actual bishops or to any meeting of the Council of Bishops is merely coincidental. But the ideas are all too real. When I read the Wesleys my heart and mind are drawn closer to God. I listen to them, I argue with them, and I submit myself to them. They are my doctrinal standard. I invite the reader to join me in this prayerful conversation with the tradition.

The Setting and Cast of Characters

It is a late night, closed door meeting of the Council of Bishops during General Conference of the United Methodist Church. Earlier that day, the General Conference overturned its longstanding opposition to homosexuality in the Social Principles. Everyone expects that tomorrow other changes to the *Discipline* regarding homosexuality will pass. In anticipation, a substantial number of conservative delegates walked out of the plenary session. They have been meeting with representatives of liberal caucuses to develop a proposal for "amicable separation." The bishops include:

- *Bishop Anchor*—a conservative who believes in maintaining the unity of the church through doctrinal agreement.
- *Bishop Compass*—President of the Council and moderator of the meeting.
- *Bishop Credo*—a conservative with ties to the evangelical caucuses who has been approached about leading a new conservative denomination if there is a separation.
- *Bishop Embrace*—a liberal with ties to the progressive caucuses who has been approached about leading a new liberal denomination if there is a separation.
- *Bishop Hound*—a cynic or a realist, depending on your perspective.
- *Bishop Leeway*—a liberal who believes in maintaining the unity of the church through reforms in the polity.

The Secret Transcript of the Council of Bishops

- *Bishop South*—a leader from one of the central conferences in the global south.
- *Bishop Temperate*—a moderate who believes in the unity of the church.

Part One

[*The bishops pause for worship after several hours of conversation. They conclude their worship by singing, "What troubles have we seen, what mighty conflicts past, fightings without, and fears within, since we assembled last!"[1] The bishops are seated.*]

Compass: We return to the urgent matter at hand. Bishop Temperate.

Temperate: Let me suggest that tomorrow we should prevent any motion regarding separation from being presented on the floor. We should rule it out of order. We should avoid the topic. Some of us should work behind the scenes and discourage delegates from bringing such a motion, but if it comes up we should kill it immediately. We were consecrated to maintain the unity of the church and it is our calling to use our authority to bury this.

Leeway: Even though I sympathize with your goal it would be a misuse of our power and would fuel deeper divisions. We need to become more inclusive by creating a more flexible structure that enables people who disagree to remain in the denomination. We must agree to disagree on this issue and we need to give conservatives and liberals alike the space they need to be true to their beliefs. Only then can we focus on those things that unite us.

---

1. *Hymnal*, 553.

The Secret Transcript of the Council of Bishops

Credo: You cannot fix this with bureaucratic changes. You are just rearranging the deckchairs on the *Titanic*. This has been a long time in coming. The actions of this General Conference call into the question whether the United Methodist Church as we know it is still part of the church of Jesus Christ. For forty years we have been fighting over the issue of homosexuality, and it has impaired our missional effectiveness. Perhaps the time has come for us to go our separate ways. This is like a dysfunctional marriage in which any further arguing is harmful.

Anchor: I can almost agree with you, except that we still have our doctrines which are constitutionally protected.[2] This is what should unite us, and we should not consider further changes to our system in order to accommodate immorality, which is the fruit of heresy. We conservatives should not leave. We should stand against this immoral decision and insist on doctrinal fidelity. But we must be prepared to be kicked out. I am afraid that our persecution is inevitable.

Embrace: Perhaps, Credo, you are right. It is time for us to go our separate ways. For years I have grieved the loss of our gay brothers and sisters who have given so much to the church. Their persecution began a long time ago. How long should someone stay in a marriage in which they are being abused?

South: This seems to be an American issue. In my conference we have much bigger concerns. If we were truly a worldwide church, would this issue take up so much time and energy?

Hound: Divorce and the Inquisition. Now there's a pair of hopeful metaphors! What are the limits of disagreement? How can we disagree and maintain true fellowship? What are the things that truly unite us? For that matter, what does it mean to be "the church" in its discipline and doctrine as well as its mission and spirituality? We have not done a very good job of helping the church talk about these issues on a level that engages our Wesleyan tradition.

---

2. *Discipline*, 29.

Compass: In this late hour we should return to our roots and listen to Wesley who also faced the issues of schism and separation. We might find in him some wise counsel for our crisis.

What is Unity?

Temperate: What would Wesley think of the phrase, "amicable separation"? It is an oxymoron. There is no such thing as a friendly divorce. I cannot imagine how separation is in keeping with the spirit of Wesley. We must redirect our attention to what truly unites us, which is our common mission in Jesus Christ. This has always united us as United Methodists. Can't we simply focus on those aspects of the mission of the church on which we all agree? As Wesley said, "Then if we cannot as yet *think alike* in all things, at least we may *love alike.* Herein we cannot possibly do amiss."[3]

Credo: What you are referring to was Wesley's understanding of Christian unity. In his sermon "Catholic Spirit" Wesley mentioned two types of union: external and "union of affection." He acknowledged that external union may not be possible (or even desirable) on issues such as style of worship.

Hound: Obviously, he was a realist about getting those old Methodists to start singing praise songs and using Power Point. The typical congregation can't unite the early service folks with the late service folks, how do we expect to keep an entire denomination connected?

Leeway: Regardless, Wesley believed in a deeper, spiritual unity that is always possible and, indeed, is already a gift given to us. He went on to describe how we should express our unity by praying for one another, encouraging one another to grow in faith and good works, and even by confronting one another with the truth in order to bring out the best in each other. As he said, "smite me

---

3. Wesley, "Letter to a Roman Catholic," 498.

friendly."[4] There is a pro-active nature to Christian unity. It is not merely a goal toward which we must strive. We must actively participate in this gift of unity in the Holy Spirit. "This is catholic or universal love," wrote Wesley, "For love alone gives the title to this character—catholic love is a catholic spirit."[5]

Anchor: But Wesley limited what he meant by "catholic spirit." He said that it is not an indifference to core doctrinal beliefs that he called "speculative latitudinarianism," which is a "great curse, not a blessing; an irreconcilable enemy, not a friend, to true Catholicism." Anyone with the true catholic spirit is "fixed as the sun in his judgment concerning the main branches of Christian doctrine." He would not settle for "muddy understanding" in order to avoid a conflict or to ignore the role of doctrine in Christian unity by "jumbling all opinions together."[6]

Isn't Tolerance Enough?

Leeway: Why can't we agree to disagree? What is wrong with having different interpretations of doctrine and differences of opinion as long as we can all get along. Our greatest strength is our pluralism. The United Methodist Church is a big tent, and the only thing we need to unite us is an agreement to respect each other, because you can believe whatever you want and be a United Methodist.

Credo: You are equating tolerance with unity. They are not the same. Tolerance is fine for a democratic society, but church unity requires more.

Anchor: Ultimately, your vision of pluralism is incoherent and contradictory. In order for pluralism to unite us, everyone must abandon their adherence to specific beliefs in exchange for complete relativism to adjudicate the conflict. In that case, respect for

---

4. Wesley, "Catholic Spirit," 91.
5. Ibid., 94.
6. Ibid., 93; compare with Wesley, "Letter to a Roman Catholic," 498–99.

real diversity is lost. For conservatives, who hold specific beliefs and practices to be essential to the faith, pluralism demands that they exchange the substance of their faith for words and symbols that mean something else or have no meaning. At best, this is a détente; at worst, it is anarchy.[7]

Temperate: While I agree that our denomination is a big tent and there is room for diverse opinions, I do not believe that pluralism is enough to unite us. The Holy Spirit unites us, not our capacity for politeness. Thus, tolerance as the centerpiece of church unity is nothing more than founding the church on human effort.

Also, there is something hallow and dishonest to say that we can have diametrically opposed interpretations about key beliefs and yet are united. If all we have to unite us is tolerance then it is a unity of the lowest common denominator and that is insufficient to keep us together, much less to effectively carry out our mission and renew the church. It would be like a dysfunctional marriage in which the spouses merely share the same house; it would be a pretense of a true covenant of marriage.

What I am saying is that there is a degree of wideness in our tradition that allows for theological diversity. How wide is that diversity? Conservatives portray the tradition as if it were a bowling lane with a narrow pathway. Instead, I think of our theological heritage like a baseball diamond from which the foul lines expand out and allow for a wider variety of fair balls to be thrown. Either way, there are certain key things that we reject.[8]

What is the Church?

Embrace: Wesley's concept of catholic spirit may help us. It reflects his understanding of the nature of the church, and even though doctrine plays a role, it is not at the center of church unity.

He often began his description of the church by expounding upon Article Nineteen of the Articles of Religion—"The visible

---

7. Abraham, "Ecumenism," 180.
8. See Morse, *Not Every Spirit*.

church of Christ is a congregation of faithful men, in which the pure Word of God is preached, and the Sacraments duly administered"—and by referencing the third century bishop Cyprian who wrote, "Where two or three believers are met together, there is a church."[9]

But then he always moved to a deeper definition of the church. In his sermon "Of the Church" he defined the "true members of the church" as those people who actively work for "unity in the Spirit in the bond of peace . . . Thus, only can we be, and continue, living members of [the] Church."[10] In short, the church equals all those members who have a "living faith."[11]

For example, this was seen in his description of baptism as an initiatory rite into the body of Christ. In baptism we "put on Christ . . . that is, are mystically 'united to Christ' and made *one* with him. For 'by one Spirit we are all baptized into one body'— namely, 'the Church, the body of Christ.' From [this] spiritual, vital union with him [comes] the influence of his grace on those that are baptized; [and] from our union with the Church [we] share in . . . all the promises Christ has made to it."[12] We are the church when we are spiritually united with other believers.

The catholicity of the church is simply "all the Christians under heaven."[13] At times, "church" refers to a small gathering of believers, and at other times, it refers to all the believers who are both living and dead. Probably the broadest term he employed was "Church of God" to refer to everything from a national church to the Methodist societies.[14] But at the heart of the church, whether it is a local congregation or the entire ecumenical movement, is this spiritual bond, a mystical union in the Spirit of Christ.

---

9. For example, Wesley "Of the Church," 46 and 51.
10. Ibid., 55–56.
11. Ibid., 51; see also, Wesley, "Earnest Appeal," 413.
12. Wesley, "On Baptism," 322.
13. Wesley, "Of the Church," 48.
14. Baker, *John Wesley*, 284–85.

Temperate: But it is unity for the purpose of making disciples. What is running through this understanding of the church is his "order of salvation"—prevenient, justifying, sanctifying grace. The church, through the sacraments and preaching, saves sinners and edifies believers. We are brought together as the church in order to receive the grace that Christ channels through the church.

Anchor: This is what he meant by "social holiness"; believers come together to support one another in the common pursuit of sanctification. He never equated "social holiness" with "social justice." However, works of justice are one part of our common, holy life.

Leeway: Obviously not every member has what Wesley called a "vital faith." His understanding of the church presupposed a distinction between what he called "scriptural Christians" and nominal Christians. The authentic church members are those whose "inmost soul is renewed after the image of God" and "who are outwardly holy, as He who hath called them is holy."[15] In contrast, he criticized "nominal Christians" who "are not now vitally united to any of the members of Christ. Though you are called a Christian you are not really a member of any Christian church. But if you are a living member, if you live the life that is hid with Christ in God" then you are a true member.[16] And so, formal statements of membership are not enough to constitute true church membership. All This reflected his goal of renewing the Church of England.

Temperate: You make Wesley sound too black and white in his understanding of church membership. Yes, he made a distinction between an "almost" and an "altogether" Christian, but he also had a porous understanding of membership. For example, his criterion For membership in the societies was only that they had a desire "to flee from the wrath to come," not that they had already achieved it.[17] Those experiencing the active working of prevenient grace

---

15. Wesley, "Principles Farther Explained," 266.
16. Wesley, "On Schism," 68.
17. Wesley, "General Rules," 69.

were included before their hearts had been warmed. Thus, the church includes those who are struggling.

Credo: Struggling, yes. They have to be at least struggling with sin, not celebrating it and tolerating it. Earlier you mentioned outward holiness, which brings up something you and Embrace are downplaying. Wesley always begins with a bare bones definition, but then he moves beyond this to a deeper definition of the church. Wesley always saw the true church or true believers as being within and visible in the institutional structure of church discipline and they are marked by personal expressions of outward holiness.

In referencing Article Nineteen and Cyprian, he made the point that the church is always visible; it is more than a "spiritual" unity. It is seen in the sacraments, heard in good preaching, and felt through the loving actions of all true believers. He had no concept of an "invisible church." If the church is the church, then it is always a visible church.

It is most visible in the holiness of its individual members and their relationships. This emphasis on holiness is reflected in his description of the church as those who are "called out" of the world.[18] We cannot avoid the issue of sexual behavior in this discussion. There is an inseparable connection between one's beliefs and one's behavior; one must claim that Jesus is Lord in one's actions.

Embrace: But Wesley also said, "The nature of religion . . . does not properly consist in any outward actions of what kind so ever."[19] By this he meant that Christianity is a religion of the heart, first and foremost, that leads to right actions. He avoided two extremes, legalism and moral indifference.

Credo: True, right behavior inevitably arises from an inner transformation. It bears fruit. What one does with his or her body is a mark of who is a true church member and who is not. By extension, when the church teaches and tolerates behavior that is not holy, then it ceases to the true church. There are four creedal marks of

18. Wesley, "Of the Church," 47.
19. Wesley, "The Way of the Kingdom," 219.

the church: one, holy, catholic, and apostolic. Right now, the mark of holiness is pitted against the mark of oneness. Thus, the issue of homosexuality strikes at the heart of the church and our unity. Homosexual behavior is clearly sinful behavior and to condone it is tantamount to surrendering our identity as the "Church of God."

Leeway: But you are putting too much emphasis on this one issue as if there is a fifth mark: straight. Your narrow litmus test ignores that the inner transformation is first and primary. The profound insight of Wesley is that right action must spring from that inner transformation. By making the issue of homosexuality into something so crucial that we should separate over it, you are obscuring this deeper unity of the Spirit who transforms us from the inside out. You are implying that what really unites us is our outward expressions of holiness rather than the source of that holiness. To put it another way, is the unity of the church so tenuous that it stands or falls on one single, outward behavior or is it the Spirit that makes us holy and unites us? The Spirit gives us the gift of unity.

Can the Church be Holy and Wrong?

Credo: At the end of the day, the only thing that matters is whether we are a scriptural church. When we stop following the Bible, then we will stop being the church. Individual members may err, single congregations may be wrong, but the church cannot err and still be the true church because it is holy, by virtue of the Holy Spirit. What may be adopted by this General Conference will set in motion a situation in which the United Methodist Church will grieve the Spirit and ultimately cease to be an expression of the true church.

Leeway: It sounds like the holiness of the church depends more on our purity and obedience than on the presence of the Holy Spirit. For the sake of argument, I will accept for a moment your premise that homosexual behavior is a sin. Even so, there are two problems with your understanding of the "holy church." First, you are assuming that church policies are at the heart of what it means to be the true church. If our policies are "holy," then we will be a holy church. This assumption is too institutional. The true church is all those believers who are united in the Holy Spirit. At best, church policies create the structures in which this can take place, but they can never prevent the Holy Spirit from making those spiritual and missional connections among believers. That is what makes us holy—the presence of the Spirit in us, in our fellowship, and in our ministry. The Spirit will always break down or defy those church structures and policies that prevent this deeper union. So even if our policies are in error, that does not disqualify the entire denomination from being a part of the "one, holy, catholic, and apostolic church."

Anchor: You are making an inaccurate assumption that the fellowship of believers is completely separate from the church as an institution. The institutional aspects of the church are interwoven with its fellowship, and they affect each other. Such a dichotomy reflects the cheap distinction often heard in society between "spiritual" and "religious." The connectional nature of our tradition assumes that the local and the general are connected. The holistic vision of Wesley will not allow for any sharp distinction between "mission" and "administration."

Leeway: Let me continue with my second point. The church is founded on the grace of Jesus Christ—which is another way of saying that the church is maintained by the presence of the Holy Spirit. The church does not exist, will not be preserved, and cannot be renewed by our acts of moral purity. There may be times when the church gets it wrong. Yet we assume that through the error, God's grace is sustaining us and God's Spirit is uniting us.

Anchor: That sounds like "cheap grace" that Bonhoeffer warned us about.[20]

---

20. Bonhoeffer, *Cost*, 43–45.

Leeway: No, it is costly for those whom God uses as a means of grace. For example, think of the former Central Jurisdiction as a theological case study. Was the Methodist Church (1939 to 1968) the church according to the marks of the creed, specifically the mark of holiness? The Central Jurisdiction was the systemic embodiment of the sin of racism; segregation was encoded into the very DNA of the denomination's constitution.[21] This was not just the racism of an individual member or local congregation; the denomination was a racist institution. And yet, I doubt if any of us are willing to say that the Methodist Church was not a part of the one, holy, catholic, and apostolic church.

I would add that during those decades of segregation, God's grace was being channeled through our members who protested the segregation and through our African American congregations who stuck it out. The gift of the Spirit was seen in this remnant band. I am not equating their story with either side in the homosexuality debate. These faithful few were the channel of grace that represented the mark of holiness. What I am saying is that the denomination can be in error on some fundamental things but still be a part of the one, holy, catholic, and apostolic church, because it is by grace that the church is saved and not by our works.

Hound: But the crucial difference between the issues of race and homosexuality is that the morality or spiritual equality of African American members was never in question. The question was

---

21. The Central Jurisdiction was created at the time of merger among the Methodist Episcopal Church (north), Methodist Episcopal Church, South, and the Methodist Protestant Church in 1939. In order for the merger to be successful, a degree of southern autonomy was preserved through the creation of a regional system of jurisdictions. In additional to geographical jurisdictions, all African American Methodist Churches were segregated into a Central Jurisdiction based on race, which ensured that southern white churches would not be served by a black pastor or overseen by a black bishop. In 1968, the Central Jurisdiction was disbanded as a part of the merger with the Evangelical United Brethren Church, but the regional system of jurisdictions remains. Bishops are elected and appointed by their respective jurisdictions and are members of their jurisdictional College of Bishops. Outside the United States, they are called central conferences.

whether that equality should be practiced in the church on earth. It should come as no surprise that Methodists have struggled longer than other mainline denominations with homosexuality because we still contain the residue of the holiness tradition, which smacks at the heart of sexuality in a way that racial segregation never did.

Credo: Leeway, are you suggesting that God will never reject the United Methodist Church? You make it sound like grace is irresistible: "once saved, always saved." Wesley must be rolling over in his grave! His understanding of the providence of God also means that if a congregation or denomination stops being faithful to the mission of Christ then God will stop using them. We have to receive God's grace by faith. To be sure, the ability to believe is a gift from God. Still, it requires a human choice. This is also the presupposition when he says that "the Church is called 'holy' because it is holy; because every member thereof is holy, though in different degrees, as he that called them is holy."[22] To your point about the Central Jurisdiction, there was a remnant of faithful believers who resisted the unholiness of the rest of the denomination. If God Rejected the denomination then those who remained faithful were the true church.

But how long will our denomination grieve the Holy Spirit by our lack of faithful obedience to God's law? At some point, it is not unreasonable to assume that God will abandon our a denomination. This in no way means that the church earns the designation "holy."

Leeway: In that case, my historical analogy of the Central Jurisdiction should give you reason to stay in the denomination when it errs so that you can be the remnant band that provides a channel of grace.

---

22. Wesley, "Of the Church," 55–56.

Part One

Can We be United in Mission?

Temperate: Both of you are wrong. The real problem of separating over this issue is that it threatens the mission of our denomination. This is the greatest threat to our identity as the church. There was a distinctively pragmatic dimension to Wesley's ecclesiology. It is in the mission of proclaiming the salvation of Jesus Christ that the spiritual unity and visible holiness of the church find their truest expressions. Listen to this wonderful quote from Wesley in which he explained the missional nature of the church:

> This is the original design of the church of Christ. It is a body of men compacted together in order, first, to save each his own soul, then to assist each other in working out their salvation, and afterwards, as far as in them lies, to save all men from present and future misery, to overturn the kingdom of Satan, and set up the kingdom of Christ. And this ought to be the continued care and endeavor of every member of his church. Otherwise he is not worthy to be called a member thereof, as he is not a living member of Christ.[23]

For Wesley, the nature of the church was wrapped up in the mission of the church, which proclaims the salvation of Jesus Christ. When this ceases to be at the center of the church then the church ceases to be.

South: But how can we "overturn the kingdom of Satan" if we have not been freed from the devil? Our mission is only effective if we have experienced and are offering the transforming power of the Gospel. And we cannot offer it if we question its truth. For years there has been a small radical minority advocating that we abandon the apostolic faith and the church's orthodox teachings on human sexuality. They are out of step with the vast majority of Christians around the world and throughout the ages.

They want to lead us down the path of further decline. Their churches are in decline in the Western and Northeastern

23. Wesley, "Reformation," 301–2.

Jurisdictions. We also know that in those places where our churches have been growing, such as the South Central and Southeastern Jurisdictions in America and in the central conferences in Africa, it is where the truth of the Gospel and the apostolic faith are being proclaimed.

Leeway: So does this mean that once we see numerical decline in those annual conferences that the apostolic faith and the church's orthodox teaching are no longer true? How do you explain the growth of some of our largest churches that are open and affirming of gays and lesbians?

Anchor: These churches have sold out to the dominant culture.

Leeway: Couldn't the same be said about our conservative churches? Aren't they riding the wave of the popularity of the Religious Right?

South: To be sure, the Gospel in the global south has been linked to certain cultural norms in order to make it relevant. Throughout the history of the church there has been a tension between two missional questions: relevancy and integrity. Making the Gospel relevant to particular cultural settings requires a process of using and transforming the ideas and symbols of the context. One the other hand, that process can go too far, and the message is fundamentally distorted when we accommodate too much of the culture. Liberals in North America claim that acceptance of homosexuality is missionally relevant, but for those who are in Africa, the opposite is true. How do we make the message relevant while maintaining the integrity of the message?

Embrace: Could it be that the African churches have accommodated the extreme prejudice against homosexuals that is in their cultures? Is that not a distortion of the message?

South: We can all agree on protecting the rights of gays and lesbians without agreeing on whether or not homosexuality is a sin.

Part One

The question before us is this: How do we remain united when the contextual demands are diametrically opposed to each other?

Anchor: I refuse to accept the premise that this boils down to regional differences, whether those differences are international or within the United States. What is right is right, regardless of the context.

When is Separation the Right Thing to Do?

Temperate: It is ridiculous to separate over one single issue. We have wasted time and energy on a few wedge issues when all of that passion could be used to confront life and death issues such as poverty and the Global AIDS pandemic.

Anchor: You are absolutely right, which is why we should have passed a resolution years ago banning any further discussion of the issue.

Embrace: For me, it is not an either-or choice between the needs of my gay and lesbian brothers and sisters and addressing those other issues. There is another missional need which all of you are ignoring: the LGBTQ community. For years we drove them out of our churches by our lack of acceptance and our conservative policies. We have perpetuated the discrimination of society through the church. We have distorted the integrity of the message of God's love by perpetuating the social sins of heterosexism and homophobia. As long as we are held captive to the wishes of the conservatives we will never be able to effectively reach this segment of the population with the love of Christ. Temperate, you make the case for unity by appealing to missional effectiveness. The same argument can be made in favor of separation. Let us go our separate ways so we can be more effective in our respective communities.

Even Wesley would approve of this form of separation based on missional necessity. He did it in 1784 when he violated the norms of church governance and ordained preachers for America. Wesley's argument for ordaining them was that he had asked the bishop of London to do it, but the bishop was too slow and then refused altogether. At that point Wesley did not want to entangle the American Methodists with Anglican authority because it would hamper their mission.[24]

Credo: But it was more than just pragmatism. He said it was "a very uncommon train of providences [which created the necessity for an American denomination and they are] at full liberty simply to follow the Scriptures and the primitive church."[25]

The linchpin for separation is fidelity to scripture and the apostolic witness. When any situation forces us to submit to an unbiblical belief or practice or restricts us from doing the mission of Christ, Wesley said that we should follow our conscience and separate. He wrote that separation is permissible "if any sinful terms of communion were imposed upon them, then they would be constrained to separate."[26]

Indeed, he said that it is our duty "totally to separate from it. Suppose you could not remain in the Church of England without doing something which the Word of God forbids, or omitting something which the Word of God positively commands; if this were the case you ought to separate from the Church of England."[27] In those circumstances the sin of separation lies with those who have made unbiblical rules.

I believe we are on the cusp of being in this position. We conservatives are on the verge of being forced to comply with "sinful terms of communion."

---

24. Robert Lowth, the Bishop of London from 1777 to 1787, nominally oversaw the colonies, but the Revolution made his authority practically ineffective. Charles Wesley had tried unsuccessfully to arrange for Bishop Seabury to perform the ordinations in America and thus prevent the creation of a Methodist denomination. Baker, *John Wesley,* 271.

25. Ibid., 253.

26. Wesley, "On God's Vineyard," 511. See also, Wesley, "The First Annual Conference," 142–43.

27. Wesley, "On Schism," 67.

Temperate: Both of you are jumping too soon to consider separation. Time and again, he opposed his own preachers who wanted to separate and denied this charge made by his opponents.

First, he advocated staying in the Church of England throughout his life. What made his critics accuse him of separation was his use of itinerant lay preachers. But as early as 1752 he required that they pledge their loyalty to remain within the Church of England, a pledge that was incorporated into the "Large Minutes" of the 1763 annual conference and was reaffirmed every year after 1773.[28]

Also, he prohibited Methodist meeting houses from conducting services during the same hours as the local parish. His bottom line definition of separation was when anyone stopped attending worship. For this reason, in the General Rules he required all Methodists to attend worship and participate in the Lord's Supper. Of course, he consistently refused to allow his lay preachers to consecrate the elements for communion.[29]

Second, he always rejected proposals for separation. Some of his lay preachers wanted to break away and form their own denomination. It was proposed and rejected at the 1755 annual conference. Again, in 1775 John Fletcher and Joseph Benson made a proposal that they launch "a daughter church of our holy mother" which reads something like our current proposals for "amicable separation." Again, Wesley would hear none of it.[30]

Even at the end of his life, he still insisted on remaining with the Church of England through a variety of sermons and tracts.[31]

---

28. John Wesley to Henry Brooke, June 1786, 332. From the beginning, the annual conference sessions were occasions for conversation to clarify the beliefs and practices of the preachers, and the minutes were the records of these doctrinal agreements. The "Large Minutes" was a compilation of the minutes of several annual conferences that summarized basic normative, beliefs and practices. It was published in 1763 but similar compilations had been used by Wesley beginning in 1749. The purpose was to provide a standard of compliance for the preachers. Heitzenrater, *People Called Methodists*, 212.

29. Wesley, "Prophets and Priests," 79.

30. Baker, *John Wesley*, 209–11.

31. For example, "On Schism", written in 1786; "On Attending the Church Service", written in 1787; "The Duty of Constant Communion", republished in 1788; "Prophets and Priests", written in 1790; "Father Thoughts", written

The Secret Transcript of the Council of Bishops

At best, he would permitted "partial" separation—withdrawing from a local parish because the priest is corrupt, whose influence may impede one's progress toward full sanctification. Regardless, Wesley believed that the sacraments are not invalidated because "unholy men" administer them. He allowed the Methodists to "quietly and silently go out of the church" when the sermon advocated predestination, but they should "attend it again [at] the next opportunity." He did not condone, however, the "general separation of the Methodists from the Church" because there was still spiritual edification to be found in the Book of Common Prayer and the Eucharist. And, with some spiritual discernment, you can even get something out a bad sermon.[32]

As for the creation of the American church, keep in mind that this separation was purely for pragmatic needs. It was not the result of a schismatic issue like we are dealing with tonight. Based on that criterion, the only reason for formal separation would be an extreme situation necessitating separate structures for the sake of advancing the mission of Christ.

The whole thrust of Wesley's relationship with the Church of England was his passionate desire to remain within it. Frank Baker rightly observes that there was an obtuseness to Wesley when he insisted that he was still loyal to the Church of England after 1784 Wesley felt torn between the church of his heritage and the effectiveness of his movement. Yet, he never saw it as an either-or choice and he never saw his actions as acts of separation. He would never approve of separation today.

Hound: So in the spirit of Wesley, we bishops should be obtuse! Our greatest strength is our missional pragmatism, as you put it Temperate. But this has also been our greatest weakness. Because we have always emphasized the pragmatic, American Methodism has always been vulnerable to being taken over by whatever is efficient. Wesley's ecclesiology is too weak to sustain us and in the

---

in 1790.

32. Wesley, "Farther Thoughts," 539; see also, Wesley, "On Attending the Church Service," 477, and Wesley, "Ought We to Separate," 339.

vacuum we have allowed the latest trends that suit our "mission" to take us over.

We are too far removed from Wesley and the original Methodists for his writings to have any relevance for our conversation tonight. Thank God, the minutes of this meeting will never be published, because if he was alive today he would sue all of you for copyright infringement for misusing his writings.

Can Doctrine Unite Us?

Anchor: That is why we need doctrinal standards and Wesley certainly included them in his understanding of church unity. There was more than just pragmatism or spirituality to his understanding of the church. Wesley's criterion for separation was more than missional effectiveness. It also includes fidelity to the truth of church doctrines.

In "Letter to a Roman Catholic" Wesley used the Nicene Creed to outline foundational doctrines.[33] Also, the Model Deed stipulated that all sermons preached in the meeting houses had to be consistent with in his *Explanatory Notes on the New Testament* and his standard sermons. This is the basis for the current definition of our doctrinal standards.[34]

Furthermore, he clearly and consistently rejected certain age-old heresies such as Arianism.[35] Even though he appealed to Roman Catholics he condemned the Council of Trent for what it said about justification. He had reservations about the condemnation of Pelagius and he did not consider the Donatists or the

33. Wesley, "Letter to a Roman Catholic," 494–96.

34. The Model Deed was the form of deed that the 1763 Annual Conference required all Methodist societies to use when purchasing property for the creation of preaching-houses. The deed stipulated that John Wesley would have free access to the property and that only preachers approved by him would be appointed to serve them. The collection of standard sermons was to function like the Anglican Book of Homilies. Heitzenrater, *People Called Methodists*, 213. See also, *Discipline*, 54–63.

35. Baker, *John Wesley*, 302.

Montanists to be heretics.[36] His tolerance of these heresies had to do with his insistence on holiness, though they may have been a little off track. However, when it comes to core doctrinal matters Wesley insisted that "men unsound in the faith, those who deny the Scriptures of truth . . . strike at the foundation" of the church.[37] If we do not have doctrinal standards we might as well pack it up!

Leeway: When I read Wesley, I am often surprised in those places where he should but does not spell out his doctrinal standards. For example, you mentioned his rejection of "speculative latitudinarianism" because it ignores "the main branches of Christian doctrine." Yet, in that sermon he did not tell us what those branches are. Furthermore, if he was really concerned about doctrinal precision, he would have kept the Athanasian Creed in his revised Book of Common Prayer when he sent it to America. No, the Apostles' and Nicene Creeds were a sufficient minimum standard; and all the other ecumenical councils were needless overkill.

Wesley affirmed essential creedal affirmations, and of course we have doctrinal standards. But they have never been at the heart of what is distinctively Wesleyan or the core of our understanding of church unity. They are a backdrop or a foundation—necessary to be sure, but never fully sufficient in themselves—for what is really at the heart of the church, which is the spiritual unity of believers in the mission of Christ. You are placing too much emphasis on doctrinal standards as a source of unity.

Hound: Okay. We all agree that we have doctrinal standards and our boy Wesley had them too. Contrary to popular opinion, you cannot believe anything you want to believe and still be a Methodist.

Yet, you misunderstand the nature of our doctrinal standards. Have you ever considered how limited those standards are either for creating unity or accountability? We have said that his *Explanatory Notes Upon the New Testament* and his standard sermons

---

36. Wesley, "Earnest Appeal," 405; Wesley, "Montanus," 485.
37. Journal entry, February 6, 1740, 263.

are part of our doctrinal standards, but have you ever read them? For example, in his New Testament *Notes,* Wesley claimed that the events prophesying the Second Coming were to happen between 1725 and 1836.[38] We missed the boat by two hundred years, doctrinally speaking, of course.

Or what about his racist comments about Native Americans in his sermon "A Caution against Bigotry," in which he writes that "it is a common thing among them for the son, if he thinks his father lives too long, to knock out his brains, and for a mother, if she is tired of her children, to fasten stones about their necks, and throw three or four of them into the river one after another."[39] Is this a doctrinal standard?

Obviously, we would all agree that Wesley was simply reflecting the cultural limitations and prejudices of his day. But from the perspective of our church law these remarks are as much a part of our doctrinal standards as everything else. With such an unwieldy source of doctrines, it becomes ridiculous to consider a church trial against a pastor for the "dissemination of doctrines contrary to the established standards of doctrine of The United Methodist Church."[40]

Embrace: There is a timeless core theme which runs throughout the doctrinal standards, a "canon within the canon," which helps us sort out what is essential from what should be left in the eighteenth century. I am referring to his "order of salvation." This was his dynamic conception of grace as prevenient, justifying and sanctifying. He referred to justification and sanctification as "fundamental doctrines" and to the schema as "three grand scriptural doctrines."[41] Typical of this is what he wrote to Thomas Church: "Our main doctrines, which include all the rest, are three, that of repentance, of faith, and of holiness. The first of these we account,

---

38. Wesley, *Explanatory Notes,* Rev. 12:16.
39. Wesley, "A Caution Against Bigotry," 67.
40. *Discipline,* 776.
41. Wesley, "On God's Vineyard," 516. See also, Wesley, "Earnest Appeal," 417.

as it were, the porch of religion; the next, the door; the third, religion itself."[42] This is the core of our doctrinal identity and unity.

Credo: It is important to note that this order of salvation presupposes the essential creedal affirmations of all Christians throughout the ages. For example, his understanding of justification makes no sense without the presupposition of the doctrine of original sin and the centrality of the atonement of Christ. The Nicene and Apostles' Creeds are the necessary foundation for Wesley's *ordo salutis*,[43] but the radical fringe, with the cooperation and support of some of our general boards and agencies, have rejected this foundation.

Leeway: But for Wesley it was never solely about a creedal affirmation. Justification and sanctification had to be experienced in order to be effective, both in the life of the individual believer as well as for the unity of the church. In fact, he was very critical of any understanding of doctrine which did not put the primary emphasis on experience. He wrote that "any religion which does not imply *the giving the heart to God*" is a false religion. It is "a religion of opinions, or what is commonly called orthodoxy. Into this snare fall thousands of those who profess to hold 'salvation by faith'; indeed all of those who by faith mean only a system of Arminian or Calvinian opinions."[44]

Even more poignant is what he said in his sermon "The Way of the Kingdom," in which he defined "true religion" as a "heart right toward God and man." And then he goes on to criticize an obsession over doctrinal standards:

> "I say of the *heart*. For neither does religion consist in *orthodoxy* or *right opinions;* which, although they are not properly outward things, are not in the heart, but the understanding. A man may be orthodox in every point; he may not only espouse right opinions, but zealously defend them against all opposers; he may think justly

---

42. Wesley, "Principles Farther Explained," 227.
43. Latin, "order of salvation."
44. Wesley, "The Unity of the Divine Being," 66.

Part One

concerning the incarnation of our Lord, concerning the ever blessed Trinity, and every other doctrine contained in the oracles of God. He may assent to all the three creeds—that called the Apostles', the Nicene, and the Athanasian—and yet 'tis possible he may have no religion at all, no more than a Jew, Turk, or pagan. He may be almost as orthodox as the devil . . . .. and may all the while be as great a stranger as he to the religion of the heart."[45]

Doctrinal standards cannot unite us because they were never meant to unite us on the deeper level that Wesley envisioned.

Credo: It was never an either-or choice for Wesley. As the leader of a renewal movement within the Church of England, he saw the Methodists as a force for reclaiming, not replacing, the spiritual potential contained in the doctrinal standards. Three hundred years later, American Methodists—on all sides of the aisle—have swung too far in the direction of the religion of the heart and are ignorant about our doctrines and their potential for renewal and unity. This is the inevitable result of the long process of liberalism that focused first on the experience and then dropped the doctrinal moorings of that experience. In the end, all you have is an amorphous feeling that often degenerates into narcissism. A rejuvenation of our doctrinal standards is both essential to the nature of the true church and for the spiritual renewal of the church. Our doctrinal standards enable us to test the spirits to ensure that the renewal we are experiencing is from the Holy Spirit and is not just the zeitgeist of our contemporary situation.[46]

Hound: But our doctrinal standards are not under attack. They are protected by the Restrictive Rules in our Constitution, and no one is advocating that we abandon the Articles of Religion or Confession of Faith. Let's face it, doctrine cannot unite us because we don't know our doctrines. The average United Methodist pastor

---

45. Wesley, "The Way of the Kingdom," 220–21.
46. I John 4:1–3.

The Secret Transcript of the Council of Bishops

can quote more lines from *The Blues Brothers* than from Wesley's standard sermons. All of this talk about doctrines is a red herring.

Leeway: I affirm the creeds and our doctrinal statements, but we may be talking past each other. We disagree on what we affirm in those creeds. The creeds use symbolic and metaphorical language that reflects their own historical situations. We need to interpret and update them for today. We cannot apply them to church life in binding or legalistic ways. Their primary purpose is formational, not judicial. Therefore, I see no contradiction between my affirmation of our doctrinal standards and my affirmation of homosexuals.

Embrace: The fullness of God's truth cannot be contained in one particular type of doctrinal expression. This is why the Bible contains a wide variety of perspectives and the unifying factor is Christ. The role of doctrine is to help the church better express "the wisdom of God in its rich variety."[47] God's truth in Jesus Christ requires a variety of expressions and to limit it to one or two creeds or to one particular historical period in the life of the church is to make an idol out of our doctrinal standards.

Anchor: You are on the slippery slope of post-modernist thinking in which anything can have any meaning. The result is that the creeds signify nothing and have no meaning. Our doctrinal standards have a normative content. They are more than just metaphors.

Credo: Because doctrine is foundational for the identity of the church, the visible unity of the church is dependent upon an official agreement on church teaching and discipline. They are under attack by those who misuse the ideas of "inclusiveness" and "tolerance" in order to distort the doctrines and discipline of our denomination. The Confessing Movement said it best: "Unity in the truth of Christ is critically dependent on unity in doctrine."[48] Even if we don't know our own standards then that only means

---

47. Ephesians 3:10.
48. "Unity In Christ," *We Confess*, 3.

Part One

that we have done a lousy job of teaching and practicing them. Our sloth doesn't diminish their importance.

Leeway: But the issue of homosexuality does not rise to the level of doctrine! Where is it mentioned in the Articles of Religion? Which paragraph addresses it in the Confession of Faith? I don't recall Wesley dealing with it, nor the ecumenical councils. It may threaten the well-being of the church, but not the essence of it. It is a non-essential issue, an "opinion" as Wesley would call it, and as such we should be tolerant of our differences. "Then if we cannot as yet *think alike* in all things," he advised, then "at least we may *love alike*. Herein we cannot possibly do amiss."[49]

But even on those issues, which we all acknowledge are core doctrinal affirmations, Wesley was willing to be tolerant of error as long as the spiritual unity is visible in our love for one another and in our common mission. Consider his view of those congregations where "the pure Word of God" is not preached, and "the sacraments are not duly administered." At first, he seemed to acknowledge that they are not a part of the universal church, but then he did not exclude them. In "Of the Church" he stated that "I dare not exclude from the Church catholic all those congregations in which any unscriptural doctrines . . . are sometimes, yea, frequently preached." He then gave the Catholics as an example of this, but went on to say of them and others, "whoever they are that have 'one Spirit, one hope, one Lord, one faith, one God, and Father of all,' I can easily bear with their holding wrong opinions, yea, and superstitious modes of worship."[50]

In his sermon "A Caution against Bigotry" he explored the meaning of Mark 9:38–39 in which Jesus tells his disciples to accept the ministries of those who "followeth not us." He went through a list of possible things which divide us, from "religious opinions" to modes of worship, and said that others "followeth not" the Methodists and yet were still true believers. The sermon climaxed by raising the question about whether we should accept the members

---

49. Wesley, "Letter to a Roman Catholic," 498.
50. Wesley, "Of the Church," 52.

"of a church as we account to be in many respects antiscriptural and antichristian . . . utterly false and erroneous in her doctrines" as true Christians.[51] And the answer was yes.

Indeed, he was willing to tolerate people in the church who are completely off base and yet share our common mission because "the hand of God is in this very thing! Even in this his wonderful wisdom appears, directing their mistake to his own glory."[52]

Unity must be visible, but it is visible in our working together, not in the words we say together. We need a new structure that enables us to "love alike" without requiring us to "think alike" on the matter of homosexuality. Right now, our connectional system forces us to move together or stay put together to the detriment of our fellowship and our mission. Tomorrow, we need to offer a proposal for a new form of connectionalism which will allow for flexibility. There are other forms of church government from which we can learn. Maybe we should reconsider the whole thing from itinerancy on down. The Presbyterians are a "connectional system" and let's be honest, the 1784 ordinations were essentially a presbyterial form of ordination. Maybe we can learn something from the Presbyterians.

[*A loud and unified gasp is heard throughout the room. A retired bishop faints. After several minutes of fanning him with a copy of the Discipline, he is revived and the conversation resumes.*]

Anchor: Leeway, you are misquoting Wesley. He was referring to ecumenical relations, not unity within a denomination which requires a covenant of discipline. Of course there are true believers in other churches that believe in false doctrines. Even so, that is different from being united in the same denomination.

---

51. Wesley, "A Caution Against Bigotry," 71.
52. Wesley, "Of the Church," 56.

Part One

Should Methodism Exist?

Temperate: Wesley's definition of the "Church of God" renders all denominational boundaries relative and provisional. He never envisioned the Methodists to be a new denomination, and it was never his desire that they become one. He wanted the Methodist movement to always remain a renewal movement within the Church of England and he hoped, in vain, that Methodism would spread into other communions as a renewal movement.[53] The "chief design" of the Methodists was "to quicken our brethren" to preach "to the lost sheep of the Church of England" and then also to the rest of the universal church.[54]

For him, it was the providence of God that had brought the movement into existence. Separation would violate God's "grand design" and "peculiar glorying" in the Methodist renewal movement. He pointed to the Moravians as a warning sign of what happens to the vitality of a movement that becomes a separate denomination. For Wesley, if the Methodists ever became a separate denomination it would be "a direct contradiction to [God's] whole design in raising them up; namely, to spread scriptural religion throughout the land, among people of every denomination, leaving everyone to hold his own opinions and to follow his own mode of worship."[55] He envisioned a pragmatic and missional unity created by God. His blessing of the American Methodist to create a new denomination was a necessity because of the limitations created by the Revolution.

Hound: If we go back to Wesley's original intention then we should not exist. So we are the bastard child of Anglicanism. Do you think they would be willing to take us back?

---

53. Baker, *John Wesley*, 316.
54. Wesley, "Ought We to Separate," 336.
55. Wesley, "On God's Vineyard," 511. See also, Wesley, "Ought We to Separate," 337, and Wesley, "Reasons Against Separation," 335–36.

Temperate: He was a pragmatist and he understood that just as God had done an extraordinary thing by raising up the Methodists in the 1740s, so too is God capable of using us in a new way today.

Embrace: It does raise the question about why we should continue to exist. What difference does it make to the larger catholic church that there is a Methodist branch?

Anchor: Wesley said that our contribution to the universal church is our understanding of the dynamics of grace, specifically the relationship between justification and sanctification as laid out in his order of salvation. He criticized Luther for neglecting the doctrine of sanctification and criticized various Catholic writers for confusing sanctification and justification. The unique contribution of the Methodists was "a full and clear knowledge of each and the wide difference between them." God gave the Methodists the right understanding of the relationship between justification and sanctification. "They maintain with equal zeal and diligence the doctrine of free, full, present justification on the one hand, and of entire sanctification both of heart and life on the other—being as tenacious of inward holiness as any mystic, and of outward as any Pharisee."[56]

Hound: Well, I am sure the Lutherans will be relieved to hear that we can help make them holy.

Three Choices: "A Way Forward", "Amicable Separation", or A Non-Stance

Compass: Should we go the way of the Evangelical Lutheran Church of America? What can we learn from the example of the Presbyterians? What happens with our relationships across the globe if we go down the path of the Episcopalians? We can all agree that advancing the mission of Christ is at the heart of the church.

---

56. Wesley, "On God's Vineyard," 506–7.

Part One

As Wesleyans, we all put a premium on doing what is pragmatic. So, enough theory. Where do we go from here?

Temperate: Let me go on record as saying that I think separation is not the answer. I agree with the statement "A Way Forward" which wisely counseled that separation "would be shortsighted, costly, detrimental to all of our churches, and not in keeping with God's will." I value the insights of both progressives and evangelicals. I believe that our denomination is richer and better equipped for mission because we have both elements in our church. We should be united by what we hold in common and not allow our differences on this issue to create a wedge so deep that it impairs our mission. I worry that if we continue on our current course that the younger generation, which is increasingly more tolerant of homosexuality, will be turned off by our all-or-nothing stance. "A Way Forward" said it best: "What makes us United Methodist is not our position on homosexuality, but a core set of theological, missional and ministry convictions. To be United Methodist is to believe, follow and serve Jesus Christ."[57]

I have been to a number of General Conferences, as you have, and we can all agree that General Conference is not equipped or capable of creating unity on this issue. There is just too much diversity at the local level. And so we should honor the work of the Spirit and the wisdom of the local church. Things need not be so centralized in order for us to still be connectional. General Conference has been moving in this direction through a wide variety of changes in the *Discipline* over the past thirty years. And so, there is past precedence to recommend the same course of action on this issue. A little flexibility would be good for all of us.

Why not allow local churches to decide whether or not they will conduct gay marriages? Those who do not want to do them will simply affirm our current stance, and those that want to offer it will be allowed to do so. We do not even need to change our statement in the Social Principles, just allow an exception for those

---

57. "A Way Forward."

churches that disagree with it. The Discipline could outline a fair process for every local church to vote on it.

Why not allow annual conference boards of ordained ministry to determine whether they will ordain gay candidates? To be sure, this would require a major change in the *Discipline*. But why not acknowledge the regional differences? Why should Rocky Mountain abide by the same standards as South Carolina? Our ordination process should acknowledge the different missional needs of each annual conference. This would make our structure truly missional.

No one would be forcing the issue on anyone. We would give every local church the right to refuse an openly gay pastor. It may make sense for a small rural church to refuse such an appointment, but why keep a good pastor from being able to serve an inner city church that would welcome a gay pastor? Obviously, we bishops would have to do the most changing. We would have to relinquish some of our authority. I, for one, would welcome it. I am tired of having to carry all the authority for holding our system together.

We need to honor the best of each side in this debate, and the best way to do this is to empower the local church to pursue the kind of ministry that best suits their unique situation. "We will be bound together by what we share in common, rather than posturing to impose our will upon one another in areas where we are so deeply divided," as the statement wisely observes.[58]

Credo: Your radical center is an illusion and a distortion of Wesley. "A Way Forward" is nothing more than a one-sided surrender to the liberal dissenters. What you are proposing means that conservatives do all the giving. Worst of all, it would be rewarding the bully tactics of leftist fringe caucuses.

Leeway: I like it as much as you hate it! As someone who sympathizes with those on the so-called leftist fringe, I think we need more flexibility so we can reach a younger generation and pursue ministry that fits our unique, local situations.

---

58. Ibid.

Embrace: It is tempting, but there are some serious problems and unanswered questions in what Temperate is proposing.

First, you are making a very big assumption that the local church is wiser and more virtuous than the Connection. You assume that giving the local church the option to vote will foster greater focus on missions. I do not believe it will. I think the unintended consequence will be that the cancer of arguing will spread. To a degree, it is contained at General Conference; General Conference appears as a distant and ridiculous rumble to the local church. If we give local churches the *option* to vote, many congregations will assume that they *must* vote. This issue, which is convoluted and lies buried in the local church, will come to the surface. Instead of arising through personal relationships, the stratospheric politics of General Conference will descend upon the local church. People who have been members of the same congregation for years will feel forced to take sides. The ambivalent feelings they have will be mishandled by incompetent pastors and strident lay leaders. The nuances and ambiguities of this issue needs to be delicately handled with pastoral wisdom. Creating an option in the *Discipline* for a congregational vote will give license to misuse it. It will turn a pastoral issue into a legal one. There is something you cannot legislate: common sense and good judgment. The unintended consequence of your romantic notions of the local church will be that the animosity could spread.

Hound: I echo your concern. I have a good friend who is a Lutheran pastor at a small church in rural Wisconsin. In his context, there was no missional urgency to deal with the issue, no gay community in his little town that needed such a witness. And yet, because his denomination allowed churches to vote on separation he had a couple of anxious, angry members who forced the issue in that little church. It meant that folks who had gotten along with each other for years suddenly had to come out on one side or the other. In the end, the church stayed in the denomination, but it caused much pain and loss. It just was not worth it.

I think there is another problem with your proposal. Giving local churches the right to refuse an appointment will violate the very nature of itinerancy. It cannot be done because of the Restrictive Rule in the Constitution.[59] Even if we want to make this change, our hands are tied.

Embrace: And, if you give a congregation the right to refuse a gay pastor, why not give them the right to refuse a woman? They will refuse a single pastor in the name of evangelism because they will be convinced that they need a pastor with a young family in order to attract a younger generation. I fear that this proposal will also lead to discrimination against LGBTQ pastors. They will be treated like second-class citizens.

Temperate: Can we not create a new version of itinerancy? This would not be the first time our itinerant system has been radically changed. Our ancestors would not recognize our current system. I think there is a way to create flexibility and maintain the connectional nature of our ministry.

Hound: Good luck getting General Conference to do it.

Temperate: We can remain connectional and still honor the uniqueness of each local church. Consider, for example, having non-geographical conferences. A conservative church in California could affiliate with a conservative jurisdictional conference and a progressive church in Alabama could unite with other liberals in a progressive jurisdiction. With modern technology location is not a limitation. We should trust conference boards to exercise good discernment to determine the right kind of pastoral leadership that is needed for their area. Let the mission of each local area drive the decision-making.

Anchor: If we cannot be united on something as foundational as the ethical standards of our pastors, then we are not united. This is a matter of integrity. When we compromise for the sake of being relevant then we are distorting the Gospel message. In the end, the mission is undermined. I can understand giving conference

---

59. *Discipline*, 29.

boards flexibility on other matters, but sexual ethics is universal. To reduce the issue to nothing more than regionalism is simply a form of relativism.

Leeway: I sympathize with the idea of creating non-geographical conferences. Yet, how can we ever define the theological difference between a "conservative" and "liberal" or an "evangelical" and a "progressive" without falling into one-dimensional stereotypes?

Credo: All this talk about regional differences and local options is just putting lipstick on a pig. We are not united, schism has already taken place according to Wesley's definition. So let us be honest. Let us have integrity. An amicable separation is the only path. For the sake of the mission of the church, let us go our separate ways and as two separate denominations we will still find ways to collaborate on those things we have in common. Why couldn't, for example, UMCOR be affiliated with both denominations? Perhaps we can continue to share the same pension plan. Those things we can agree on, but for the sake of the mission we should go our separate ways in order to be more effective just like Paul and Barnabas did.

Of course, it will be very difficult to sort out the administrative details of such a separation. Seminaries and other related institutions could be given the option of who to affiliate with. Why not dual affiliation? As for our general boards and agencies, it is high time we undergo radical restructuring. Some of them need to die. Perhaps amicable separation will provide the unintended gift of streamlining our respective systems so that more outreach can be done.

What do we have to lose? Endless debates at General Conferences? Repeated church trials?

If you are right and our current stance is a hindrance for reaching a younger generation—which I doubt—then you should agree with me, brothers and sisters.

Hound: There's nothing like the competition of a sibling rivalry to fuel evangelism!

The Secret Transcript of the Council of Bishops

Leeway: It sounds tempting but I am not convinced that the denomination would divide so neatly. This issue does not simply divide along regional lines but right down through every congregation, every household. Individuals do not fall into neat categories of "liberal" and "conservative" even on this issue.

In one of the local churches I served there were two women who had adopted five children out of foster care, most of which had been born to addicted mothers. They were good, devoted mothers who truly embodied the way of Jesus in their compassion for their children. They were also lesbians who never announced or discussed their relationship in public, even though it was obvious to all when I baptized their kids. So, one day during the Presidential elections I pulled into the church parking lot and there on back of their minivan was a McCain-Palin bumper sticker. It did not make sense to me until I talked with them and discovered that they were passionately opposed to abortion. They had taken in these children and the thought of abortion was a violation of their calling to be mothers.

So I ask you: Where do pro-life lesbians go to church? They would never feel comfortable in either a liberal or conservative Methodist denomination. But they still have a home in the United Methodist Church with our weird and eclectic diversity.

South: I am afraid that the time and energy it takes for you Americans to divide up the denomination will take resources away from advancing the Gospel among my people. All this talk about being freed up for missions could backfire. How much money and time will be lost in getting everything divided? The unintended consequence of separation may be a loss in mission work.

Credo: There is an historical precedent for amicable separation. Wesley separated from George Whitfield and the Calvinist Methodists over a core doctrinal issue and yet they found ways to work together from time to time.[60]

---

60. Baker, *John Wesley*, 126–29: Best, *Charles Wesley*, chapter 6; Williams, *John Wesley Today*, 154–55.

Part One

Temperate: Still, Wesley clearly counseled against separation from the Church of England because the core doctrines and liturgy were not at issue.

Credo: Wesley fostered the separation of American Methodists from the Church of England.

Temperate: But that was a geographical necessity. He resolutely refused the same option for British Methodists who could receive the Eucharist in their parishes.

Hound: So it depends on which historical example you want to use to further your cause.

Credo: The only reasonable way forward that has integrity for all sides is amicable separation. I take the liberal caucuses at their word. They have no intention to compromise and I am not asking them to. They should not have to compromise their beliefs any longer. So like Paul and Barnabas, we should go our separate ways. When we can cooperate we will but let us not act as if we are united when we are not.

Hound: We will not divide but splinter. True to the history of Protestantism, those who leave will have divisions among themselves. There will be a Conservative Methodist Church and then an Ultra Conservative Methodist Church and a Moderate Conservative Methodist Church. There will be Liberal Methodist Church and a Progressive Liberal and a Moderate Progressive and so forth. Just imagine the initials—CMC, UCMC, MCMC, LMC, PLMC, MPMC! We are too old for all that changing.

Why do we need to take any stance on this issue? The current cultural and political climate demands that everyone take sides, but the church is called to be separate from these dynamics. Yet, we mainline Methodists have been so deeply entrenched in American culture and its fading version of Christendom that we assume that we must take a stance on every contemporary issue. We must be "relevant" and "responsible." But now in the twilight of Christendom we are an afterthought in American culture. With that disestablishment comes a peculiar gift. We do not have to assume responsibility for the culture wars; we do not have to let society's agenda dictate the course of our prophetic witness. We do not need to take a stand, for or against or anything in between, on the issue of homosexuality. When we stop mimicking society we can truly learn how to be the church. Besides, no one cares what we think.

What might a non-stance look like? One, we would strip all references to homosexuality from the *Discipline*. We would prohibit our general boards and agencies from issuing any statements, funds or resources that involve this issue. However, our denominational silence would allow for local churches and annual conferences to sort it out as the Spirit leads them. The development of liturgy would arise from the local church experience. Evangelism would rise or fall depending on how it developed among our congregations. The best thing we can do right now is to create space and silence and to let the world pass us by.

A Graceful Church

Compass: Let's pause and look at the issue again from Wesley's understanding of the church and then judge the practical issues. From a Wesleyan perspective, the church—whether it is a gathering of two or three people or a worldwide denomination—is a visible gathering or connection of true believers who are saved and are being saved by the grace of God in Jesus Christ. The common denominator is their personal experience of the order of salvation in the Spirit of Christ which they all share. The order of salvation also implies that different church members will be at different stages of development in their faith, but membership is more than simply having your name on the rolls. This grace is channeled through our fellowship and ministries and through the proclamation of the Word and the administration of the sacraments. It is always "visible" in two ways: in the institutional denomination, which is the steward of the sacraments and doctrines, and in the fellowship, worship, witness, and good works of its members. Because

Part One

God's grace is universal and eternal, the church is universal and the believers are connected with one another throughout eternity. In short, the church's center is grace.

Here's an analogy: Do you remember the road trip we took during the General Conference in Pittsburgh? We drove out to see Frank Lloyd Wright's house Fallingwater. You will recall that the house sits astride a waterfall, obviously the worst place to build a house. Yet it remains standing because the foundation is a gigantic slab of stone that is naturally cantilevered over the waterfall. Wright used the cantilever as a theme throughout the house. Everything from the balcony to the bookshelves is cantilevered.

Wesley's concept of grace is the unifying theme that runs throughout his conception of the church. The various parts, which at times seem to be at odds with each other, are connected by the grace of God. And so, the unity of the church is God's gift of love in Christ.

If grace is the blueprint of God's house, then the link between our doctrines and our spiritual communion is the reality of God's saving grace. The former bears faithful witness to the latter and the latter makes the former effective and edifying to the church. Doctrine alone does not unite us, but doctrine is a reliable description of the Holy Spirit who unites us, and, in turn, doctrine helps support our unity.

And like Wright's cantilevered house, grace often feels like a precarious foundation for the church. We are tempted to replace this graceful foundation with our efforts. The net effect is that more is less. We cannot save the church, only God can. We cannot unite the church; we can only receive the gift of unity. We exist collectively by the grace of God, and whatever happens tomorrow will not, cannot, diminish God's grace in Jesus Christ.

The gift of unity is for the mission of the church. Our unity is a means to the greater end of sharing the salvation of Jesus Christ. Our pluralism and diversity are necessary, but they are not the goal. They are tools to help us achieve the mission of making disciples for the transformation of the world.

Our unity takes the shape of concentric circles. The outer circle includes the doctrinal standards and discipline of the institutional church. For Wesley, these are accurate representations of and essential resources for the inner, spiritual unity of believers. But alone they are useless, and perhaps even misleading, giving people a false sense of what it means to be a Christian. The inner circle is the spiritual union of all true believers in the Spirit of Christ. Because the definition of a true believer is anyone who has the Spirit of Christ animating his or her life, the definition of the true church are all those believers connected in the Spirit of Christ. But this spiritual union is faithfully transmitted to us through scripture and tradition, and it is faithfully expressed through our works of piety and mercy.

It is our lack of faith in God's grace to sustain and save the church which tempts us to fill in this inner circle with what properly belongs on the perimeter. Are we not trying to "save" our precious denomination by our bureaucratic maneuvering, doctrinal purity, evangelistic gimmicks, and inclusivity? It is a form of ecclesial Pelagianism. We are trying to save the Church through our works, be they doctrinal, evangelistic, or political.

It truly is an act of faith to assume that the Spirit of Christ is in the hearts of those who sit beside us in the pew and those who sit across from us in our debates. Paul said it best, "For by grace you have been saved through faith, and this is not your own doing . . . For we are what he has made us, created in Christ Jesus for good works, which God prepared beforehand to be our way of life."[61] The "we" in that passage is the church. And, like it or not, God has stuck us together in this house so that we can work together to do all the good we can in Christ Jesus.

Hound: Well, it's time for me to go to the bathroom in the household of God.

---

61. Ephesians 2:8, 10.

Part Two

[The bishops take a restroom break. After several minutes they resume their conversation.]

What Should be Our Membership Standards?

Compass: I believe we are all back.

Credo: While we were taking a break, I was thinking about your beautiful description of the church as the household of God's grace. But the issue of homosexuality brings up a variety of unpleasant things that need to be repaired in God's household.

I am referring to our membership standards. A few years ago this group issued a pastoral letter regarding Judicial Council decision 1032[1] in which we affirmed that "homosexuality is not a barrier" to membership and we called upon all of our pastors and churches "to make every congregation a community of

---

1. The case involved a Virginia pastor who refused membership to an openly gay man who was unwilling to renounce his homosexual behavior. The bishop and the members of the clergy session of the annual conference placed the pastor on involuntary leave of absence for "unwillingness or inability to perform ministerial duties." Decision 1032 overturned their decision and reinstated the pastor. The rationale of the decision was that the pastor is "solely responsible for making the determination of a person's readiness to receive the vows of membership. The vows of membership for uniting with a United Methodist church (¶ 217) are detailed and explicit." Judicial Council, "Decision 1032."

hospitality."[2] While I still stand by my decision to sign that letter, I need to clarify what I understood it to mean.

First, homosexuality as a sexual orientation has never been a barrier to membership. We love the sinner and we want to welcome all sinners into the church, but with the goal that our hospitality will lead them to repent of their sins. It is homosexual behavior that we condemn. It is their persistence in acting on these desires which demonstrates that they are not ready to profess our membership vows with integrity. It is different if a homosexual is trying to resist these desires—a sign of prevenient grace at work, to be sure—but if they are unapologetic about their behavior, then we know they are not serious.

Second, we have always had and continue to have membership standards. It is ludicrous to suggest that pastors are required to accept into membership anyone who says they want to be a member. For example, the 1860 Discipline described a probationary membership period for the laity.

Compass: We are well acquainted with the list of examples that you shared with us several hours ago.[3]

Credo: Let me just summarize by saying that every pastor, liberal and conservative alike, judges the "readiness" of prospective members and they practice some form of membership requirements, be they explicit or implicit. From a purely organizational perspective, no organization can exist for very long unless it has some minimal membership guidelines.

Embrace: I think you are setting up a works righteousness based on a person's sexual orientation. This is nothing more than the narrow ideology of the Religious Right being imposed on our membership standards. The United Methodist Church is an open and inclusive church. "Open Hearts, Open Minds, Open Doors" was more than a media slogan; it was a challenge for us to live out what we have said in Article Four of our Constitution. This is

---

2. Council of Bishops, "Pastoral Letter."
3. Case, "Historic Review," 4–5; "United Methodism's Vows at Risk," 9.

Part Two

more than regurgitated liberal tolerance. It is Wesley's insistence on God's grace being extended to all people. "Come, sinners, to the Gospel feast; let every soul be Jesus guest; ye need not one be left behind, for God hath bid all humankind!"[4]

Credo: Yes, but we come as *sinners* to that feast! In essence, do we take seriously the question: "Do you renounce the spiritual forces of wickedness, reject the evil powers of this world, and repent of your sin?"[5]

Embrace: But Wesley would never have created a litmus test of doctrines and minor biblical disputes. Look at our understanding of open communion, which comes directly from Wesley's insistence that the only preparation for the Lord's Supper was spiritual hunger, not doctrinal purity. Our stance on open communion embodies our vision of being an inclusive denomination.[6]

The requirements for membership should be basic: confess faith in the Trinity and seek to bear the fruits of the Spirit.

Credo: You mischaracterize Wesley's standards for membership in a class meeting. Yes, there were no doctrinal affirmations. But practicing the discipline of the General Rules was no easy thing. Members were regularly corrected and even denied participation in the love feasts and removed from membership.[7] It was inclusive for anyone who had the desire to progress in their faith. It was intolerant of anyone who was unwilling to submit to the discipline of growing in grace. In short, they had to be fleeing sin, not bringing it with them and expecting the church to bless it.

---

4. *Hymnal,* 616. Article Four states: "The United Methodist Church acknowledges that all persons are of sacred worth. All persons without regard to race, color, national origin, status, or economic condition, shall be eligible to attend its worship services, participate in its programs, receive the sacraments, upon baptism be admitted as baptized members, and upon taking vows declaring the Christian faith, become professing members in any local church in the connection." *Discipline,* 24.

5. *Hymnal,* 34.

6. Resolution 8032, "This Holy Mystery," 961–64.

7. Ruth, *Little Heaven,* 103–4, 112–16.

Temperate: Bishop Embrace is not saying that there should be no membership standards, only that those standards should focus on what are absolutely essential expressions of faith. You are questioning whether Embrace's definition is too minimal, which is a legitimate concern.

God knows that we have watered down the meaning of membership for too long. For decades we lowered the bar in order to fit into American middle class culture. We have baptized too many children only because we wanted to make the grandparents happy. And now we are so desperate to regain the glory days of numerical growth that we are willing to take in anyone who shows any interest in us. Ironically, it takes longer to get removed from the rolls than it does to get on them. The net effect makes our membership vows almost meaningless.

But you can err in the other direction too. If we make our membership standards too stringent, then it leaves no room to accept people who are not mature in their faith. Wesley acknowledged that there are degrees of faith, and we should be willing to take people in as members who are at a variety of stages in their faith development.[8]

Any true renewal of our denomination will be reflected in a new understanding of membership. Somehow, we need to learn on a practical level how to combine the inclusiveness of Wesley's understanding of grace with his insistence on growing in grace through relationships of support and accountability. And it is not just church membership that needs to embody this balance. We struggle with this issue every time we must discipline a pastor who has gotten in trouble. If we are experiencing real spiritual renewal then we will neither sweep those problems under the rug nor will we abandon them. There are days when I cannot find that balance.

Hound: The real question is whether our stance on homosexuality is integral to our membership standards. The preface to the Social Principles suggests otherwise when it states that they "are intended

---

8. On degrees of faith and regeneration see Wesley, "Principles," 64; Collins, *Scripture Way,* 107–10.

to be instructive and persuasive in the best of the prophetic spirit; however, they are not church law." At best, when the *Discipline* outlines our membership standards it says that the "Social Principles shall be considered as an essential resource for guiding each member of the Church in being a servant of Christ on mission."[9] "Essential resource" and "guiding" are hardly the language of mandatory compliance.

Are we really willing to implement all of the Social Principles? To be honest, no one pays attention to the *Discipline's* definition of membership. We should start practicing what we preach. We have members who are business leaders who routinely violate our social teachings on labor relations. For that matter, how many of us sit on the boards of church-related institutions which engage in union busting, though our Social Principles affirm workers' rights? What about all those lay members who have supported war even though it contradicts the Social Principles: "We therefore reject war as an instrument of foreign policy."[10] President Bush, a United Methodist layman, led us into war even though he violated our Confession of Faith, which declares that "We believe war and bloodshed are contrary to the gospel and spirit of Christ."[11] Where was the heresy trial of the President?

It is not just the laity. Pastors are sworn to a covenant of ministry that they violate all the time. If keeping covenant means complying with the *Discipline*, then it means keeping the whole thing. Thus, a pastor violates the covenant every time he or she fails to complete the charge conference forms. All this talk of violating the covenant smacks of hypocrisy.

But the alternative is no better. We can put the accent mark on the preface of the Social Principles and say that we will not bar violators from membership. But that simply means that we are a church that is unwilling to live by our convictions. This is cynicism—affirming those things we have no intention to do. This has been our mode of operation for too long. We have made

9. *Discipline*, 154.
10. Ibid., 140.
11. Ibid., 75.

the question, "Do you renounce the spiritual forces of wickedness, reject the evil powers of this world, and repent of your sin?", meaningless.

The liberals are inconsistent when they promote the Social Principles on everything from global warming to the death penalty but encourage disobedience on the issue of homosexuality. You cannot have it both ways. So we are stuck between hypocrisy and cynicism.

Leeway: This illustrates my point that the issue of homosexuality does not rise to the level of doctrine, and therefore cannot be a barrier to membership. Because our Social Principles do not carry the same authority as our doctrinal standards these ethical issues, which vary and change over time, do not carry the same weight as the essential confession of Jesus Christ as Lord. Homosexuality is a non-essential thing that should not divide us.

How Does a Homosexual Experience Grace?

Credo: But it does rise to the level of doctrine by virtue of what Embrace said earlier was the core of our doctrinal standards: Wesley's order of salvation. Earlier, we agreed with Bishop Compass's apt description that grace is the center of the church's identity and mission. We also agreed that, as Wesleyans, the grace of God in Jesus Christ is understood as prevenient, justifying and sanctifying grace. The *Discipline* says it best, "Grace pervades our understanding of Christian faith and life . . . While the grace of God is undivided, it precedes salvation as 'prevenient grace,' continues in 'justifying grace,' and is brought to fruition in 'sanctifying grace.'"[12] This order of salvation is both our doctrinal core and the lived experience of every church member. From a Wesleyan perspective, it is never enough to affirm this concept of grace in the abstract. It must be experienced; it has to become a reality for each believer. So you could say that this concept of grace is where the doctrinal and the ethical intersect. There is continuity from orthodoxy to

12 *Discipline*, 45–46.

Part Two

orthopathy to orthopraxis. What we do with our bodies directly reflects what we believe with our minds. The issue of holiness is so central to Wesley that you cannot disconnect beliefs from actions. Thus, you cannot dismiss an ethical issue by saying it is on a lower level than doctrine.

Now, we have consistently said that homosexuality is "incompatible with Christian teaching."[13] Homosexual desires and actions are sinful. Our membership standards are very clear that if you are going to join the United Methodist Church you need to repent of your sins, "confess Jesus Christ as Savior," put your "whole trust in his grace and promise to serve him as [your] Lord."[14] To condone homosexual desires and behavior is a clear sign that you are not confessing with your life and thoughts that Jesus Christ is Lord and, therefore, you are not taking the membership vows seriously.

I know this sounds harsh, but that is only because we have become so accustomed to our society's overemphasis on tolerance. The liberals have overemphasized God's acceptance at the expense of the transformative power of the Gospel. This mistake reflects their misunderstanding of grace. Sanctification's goal of "Christian perfection" is a lifelong process of spiritual growth in our love of God and humanity. Methodists have always believed that this process of sanctification is cultivated by spiritual disciplines, which include living in a disciplined covenant with the church. This is a very ancient concept, but it runs contrary to the excessive individualism and relativism in our contemporary culture.

I am not singling out homosexuals or creating a double standard. As I said, we should not bar someone from membership because of their sexual orientation. It is their behavior that cannot be tolerated. Again, the central question: Do you repent of your sins?

Hound: Love the sinner but hate the sin?

Credo: Yes. If anyone, homosexual or heterosexual, is going to experience the blessings of sanctifying grace they must submit to a

---

13 Ibid., 111.
14. Ibid., 137.

membership covenant. But if all we do is accept them then we are actually depriving them of the fullness of salvation.

Embrace: If you are right and the liberals have failed to explain how a homosexual can be born again, then you conservatives have another problem at the other end of the process of sanctification: Can a homosexual experience Christian perfection?

You agree with the modern distinction between sexual orientation and behavior—a modern concept which is foreign to scripture—and you insist that it is only the behavior that you object to, not their orientation. Would you say that one's sexual orientation is something that cannot be changed?

Credo: I believe that sexual orientation is not biological or genetic. It is a complex mix of nurture, environment, family dynamics and choice. We are not requiring, nor should we ever require, that someone be able to change his or her sexual orientation.

Embrace: This implies that the most the LGBTQ person can hope for is to curb their actions and suppress those sexual desires. They can be celibate but never be able to experience wholeness in their sexuality. Thus, heterosexual orientation is the only way anyone can experience a "sanctified" sexuality, but if their orientation cannot be changed then they can never experience sanctifying grace. This sounds more like Luther's *simul iustus et peccator*[15] than Wesley's doctrine of perfection, which gives us hope that we can overcome sin in this lifetime.

If homosexuality is a sinful orientation, then it would seem that Christian perfection for a homosexual is the transformation of their sexual orientation. It is not just the ability to resist the desires but the actual annihilation of the orientation that produces those desires. Indeed, if salvation is the restoration of the image of God in the soul and if, as you seem to believe, that heterosexuality is rooted in creation, then sanctification can only mean that a homosexual will be given a new sexual orientation. If this is not possible, then the most they can hope for is something less than the

---

15. Latin for "simultaneously righteous and sinner."

full healing and wholeness of grace, and the only people who are capable of this are heterosexuals. In the end, this line of thinking treats LGBTQ persons as second class citizens among the people of God.

Also, you have completely misunderstood what I said about the inclusivity of the church. Our society practices a watered down form of acceptance. People are tolerated but not embraced in our society, and most of our churches confuse polite, middle class tolerance with the radical hospitality envisioned in the Gospel. In our society, LGBTQ persons are not accepted. Yes, there is a cultural shift taking place toward greater acceptance but there is still discrimination, harassment and violence against these people. They have been shunned by their families; they have been denied equal protection under the law; they have been attacked and ridiculed. And what happens when they come to our churches? They get more of the same from our official policies.

The inclusivity of the church must go beyond polite tolerance. It is the act of embracing people with the unconditional acceptance of the grace of God. When the church does this it is embodying grace, it is grace incarnated in the church as the body of Christ.

Anchor: How does this understanding of grace fit with Wesley's order of salvation? It sounds like you are watering down the distinctive Wesleyan perspective. What is justification without repentance and the forgiveness of sins? What happens to the new birth? What does it mean for a homosexual to be born again?

Embrace: I am not saying that LGTBQ persons have no sins to repent. First, it is obvious that they must repent of the same sins that everyone else commits, from anger to greed and so on. But there is a sinful dynamic they experience that is unique to their social location. Sin is more than individual transgressions. The sin is not homosexual behavior but heterosexism which holds them captive. These persons have internalized this hatred. In turn, this domination leads to unhealthy and immoral behavior, from self-destructive acts to promiscuity. These are sinful responses to a sinful context. They need to be freed from the sins of our oppressive culture. They also need forgiveness for their sinful reaction to and participation in this sin-filled context of alienation and domination.

To answer your fundamental question, the LGBTQ believer must "renounce the spiritual forces of wickedness" imbedded in our heterosexist culture, "reject the evil powers of this world" of homophobia and all other forms of oppression, and "repent of their sins" of self-destructive promiscuity and hatred.

Temperate: I think that the way Wesley described the relationship between justification and regeneration in the experience of new birth is very helpful at this point. "Justification is another word for pardon"; Wesley says, "it is the forgiveness of all our sins, and . . . our acceptance with God."[16] Justification is not a form of "fooling God" into thinking that the believer is innocent, as if Christ's righteousness blocks God's view of us as we are.[17] It is God accepting us as sinners who have been controlled by and have participated in a sinful world. We accept God's acceptance of us by renouncing the sin that has dominated our lives and asking God to forgive us for participating in that sinful situation.

Embrace: But at the heart of justifying grace is God's radical acceptance of us just as we are. For a LGBTQ person that means accepting the fact that God accepts them even though the world rejects them and tries to impose its standards on them. He or she seeks God's forgiveness for perpetuating these forms of sinful domination in themselves and their relationships.

The new birth, which is the beginning of sanctification, is a real change in the believer who is "inwardly renewed by the power of God."[18] The image of God is restored and the power of sin is removed from the believer.[19] The believer is given power over both

---

16. Wesley, "Scripture Way," 157.
17. Wesley, "Justification by Faith," 188.
18. Wesley, "Scripture Way," 158.
19. Wesley, "Original Sin" 185 and "On Sin in Believers" 321.

Part Two

inward and outward sin, a power which deepens and develops over time.[20] For LGBTQ persons this is the healing of their psyches and souls from the violence of heterosexism that they have internalized and it means abandoning self-destructive patterns of promiscuity and abuse. In short, it is a radical transformation from the inside out, but that transformation does not require changing the sexual orientation with which God created them.

Justification and the new birth are inseparably related. There is no temporal distinction between justification and the new birth, only a logical one.[21] By holding these two things together, Wesley's great insight is that we experience grace as a paradox. It is a paradox of radical acceptance and radical transformation. When we experience God's unconditional acceptance we also begin to experience God's total process of transformation.

Conservatives do not see the connection between acceptance and transformation. For someone who has always been treated as an outcast, the act of accepting them is transformative. It creates the possibility for transformation to occur. Without that acceptance the message of transformation sounds impossible and condemning. For Wesley, salvation is a restoration of the image of God in us, not a denial of who God created us to be. Because you cannot truly accept their sexual orientation, you cannot offer them true transformation into who God created them to be.

Hound: That's the weirdest interpretation of Wesley I have ever heard. I have never heard any progressive make the case the way you are stating it.

Embrace: That's the problem with the progressive caucuses. They have not taken our doctrinal standards seriously. On that score, the conservatives have been right to criticize us. Even so, conservatives do not have an exclusive claim to our Wesleyan heritage.

Credo: We conservatives see the connection between acceptance and transformation. You liberals are confusing the two. You are

20. Wesley, "Marks," 419.
21. Wesley, "Great Privilege," 431–32.

collapsing one into the other. Wesley would never agree with the direction you are taking his theology.

Anchor: What you just did with Wesley's order of salvation is a good example of why there must be more doctrinal content to our unity. Methodists need to affirm the tradition of the ancient ecumenical creeds as an anchor for a proper understanding of grace.

You are treating grace as if it is an empty concept into which you can deposit your political ideology. Grace is the very presence of the risen Son, the gift of the Holy Spirit to forgive, reassure, and transform that is given by the Father. The problem with your appeal to Wesley's *ordo salutis* is that it reduces grace to a program that we control rather than Christ controlling us.

South: At the heart of the order of salvation is a vision of the Christian life in which the believer is consumed by Christ; Christ in us and us in Christ, to die with Christ and to be raised to new life in Christ. The *ordo salutis* is not a formula or a program. Grace is the very presence of Christ forgiving, affirming, and transforming us. As Charles Wesley said, "Jesus, thine all victorious love shed in my heart abroad . . . Refining fire, go through my heart, illuminate my soul; scatter thy life through every part and sanctify the whole."[22] The soul of Methodism is this passion for Christ.

Leeway: On that we agree, but my challenge for you is this: I believe that a person's sexual orientation is no barrier to life in Christ. I have seen, like Paul and Cornelius' people, LGBTQ persons who have this passion for Christ.

Embrace: We can agree that grace is the gift of the Spirit of Christ who forgives, assures, and transforms. I disagree with your portrayal of the dynamics of grace having nothing to do with our contemporary issues. Your description of grace implies that it all takes place in a spiritual vacuum or on some kind of metaphysical level. Remember, the gift of grace was incarnated and lived among

---

22. *Hymnal*, 422.

Part Two

in the social struggles of his day; so too does his continuing presenceimpact and interact with our social struggles.

Compass: Let's cut to the chase: the difference between Credo and Embrace boils down to their different definitions of sin. Is homosexual behavior a sin or not? This is the heart of our debate. How you answer that question shapes how you understand Wesley's order of salvation.

What does the Bible Say?

Anchor: And that brings up the authority of scripture. We have been dancing around that issue all night. Wesley wrote, "I am not afraid that the people called Methodists should ever cease to exist either in Europe or America. But I am afraid, lest they should only exist as a dead sect, having the form of religion without the power. And this undoubtedly will be the case, unless they hold fast both to the doctrine, spirit, and discipline with which they first set out. What was their fundamental doctrine? That the Bible is the whole and sole rule both of Christian faith and practice."[23]

Regardless of whether the church changes its policies and doctrines, the Bible is unwavering in its condemnation of homosexuality.

Hound: Oh, good God! Here we go again, another endless debate about the Bible.

Leeway: Homosexuality is a minor topic in the Bible, and we should stop making such a big deal out of it.

South: Bestiality is a minor topic in the Bible but that does not mean we should condone it. If you accept homosexuality, where does it end?

---

23. Wesley, "Thoughts Upon Methodism," 527.

Embrace: First, the Bible never uses the word homosexuality, which is a modern psychological concept. What is being condemned is very specific behavior, such as the exploitation of younger men by older men. Second, these passages, including Romans One, should be seen in light of their historical context of idolatry. What is being condemned is exploitative forms of same-sex behavior, such as male prostitution. The biblical worldview never conceived of homosexual relationships based on mutuality and equality. The Bible is right as far as it goes, but it does not speak to the new situation we find ourselves in today.

Leeway: Also, Jesus never said anything about homosexuality, and shouldn't he be the basis for our ethics, not some obscure verse that is read out of context?

South: What the Bible says about homosexual behavior reflects the biblical principle of heterosexual monogamy as expressed in Genesis Two. This theme is a part of the doctrine of creation, and even though Jesus said nothing directly about homosexuality, he did affirm this deeper theme when he condemned divorce. Twisting Scripture to excuse homosexuality makes it more difficult for my people to understand our condemnation of polygamy.

Embrace: But affirming heterosexual monogamy does not require us to condemn homosexual monogamy. If you follow the logic of your argument, then being single is an aberration. If genital sexual relations is the basis for defining monogamy, then why not also include what Genesis says about being "fruitful and multiplying" but you can't go there because that would lead to the conclusion that you should only have sexual intercourse when you are trying to procreate.

Hound: Maybe we should adopt that stance. It might solve our membership decline.

Embrace: Besides, what do you do with all those passages about polygamy? God never condemned the Israelite kings for having multiple wives.

Part Two

South: Those are historically conditioned circumstances that do not diminish the timelessness of the biblical principle of heterosexual monogamy.

Embrace: But where do you draw the line in your biblical interpretations? There are all sorts of things that many Methodists once thought were timeless ethical teachings, from slavery to divorce, that we now recognize do not have a literal application for today.

Credo: Your position plays into the hands of relativists of all stripes. Is there no scriptural direction for the question of gay marriage?

Embrace: And your position denies all forms of historical development and the ongoing providence of God. The deeper and more fundamental principle in the Bible is mutual love. The criteria should be: Is this relationship one of fidelity and equality that exhibits the fruits of the Spirit which should be evident in all relationships?

Credo: That is too vague. Where do you draw the line? It becomes like a ball of twine that once you start unwinding it nothing is left. In terms of sexual expression, the Bible reveals that that kind of mutual love is possible only in a monogamous heterosexual relationship: traditional marriage.

Temperate: Obviously, it gets us nowhere to say that one side is scriptural and the other is not. Both sides of this debate claim to be biblical and yet you have such different approaches to Scripture because you have different views of how the Spirit of God works. One side assumes that the Spirit does new things in our age, such as the acceptance of homosexuality. Where the other side assumes that the Bible describes and limits the predictable ways the Spirit works, thus it would be out of the question that the Spirit would approve of homosexuality.

Embrace: That is my point. I believe the best biblical analogy for our current situation is the dilemma Peter faced in Acts Ten in

55

which God calls him to accept the gentiles as true believers because God is doing a new thing.

Credo: But being a gentile is not the same as being a homosexual. Unlike the scriptural stance against same-gender sexual relations, there are passages in the Old Testament that allude to the inclusion of gentiles into God's plan of salvation. Peter realized in Acts Ten. Instead, the best biblical analogy is the limitations the church placed on gentile believers in Acts 15:20; they had to renounce idolatry. Homosexuality is the result of idolatry, as Romans One describes it.[24]

Should We Perform Gay Weddings?

Compass: It all boils down to whether you define homosexual behavior as sinful or not. The burden falls on the progressives to demonstrate how gay marriage has a spiritual basis. It is insufficient to use the secular rationale that it is a civil right. This is sufficient for the courtroom, but there must be a higher standard for the church. Marriage is more than a right. It is a gift and a responsibility.

Hound: We can hardly look to John Wesley for guidance on marriage!

Leeway: Maybe Charles.

Embrace: Marriage must be offered to LGBTQ persons as a way to live out their discipleship. If covenant relationships are a means of grace, then the covenant of marriage should not be denied them for the sake of their growth in grace. To be sure, the same must be said for heterosexual believers. The same qualities of love and fidelity mark both kinds of marriage. In short, if we accept LGBTQ

---

24. For further discussion, see Furnish, "Bible and Homosexuality"; Hays, *Moral Vision*, 379–406; and Scroggs, *New Testament*.

persons into membership then we must offer them the rituals that help them grow in grace.[25]

Leeway: This is an example of the limitations of a secular argument being applied within the Church. In society, the case for gay marriage is based on equal rights. Within the Church, there is another language and logic based on responsibility and gift; it the logic of covenant-making.

Credo: This is why it should not be offered to our gay members. It will mislead them into assuming that they can grow in grace without the repentance of sin. Thus, the crux of our debate is whether homosexual practices are sinful. I am afraid that our congregations will want to offer same-sex weddings because society says it is ok. Society should not set the standards. Worse still, evangelical pastors will be required to violate their consciences and perform gay weddings. Therein lies the irony of pluralism.

Hound: But just think about how much more money we can make from wedding fees. This will solve our financial problems!

Should We Tolerate Dissent?

Temperate: The issue is not who is right. The issue is whether we can live with various interpretations of scripture and still be united as a church.

South: Are you suggesting that all interpretations are relative? If that is the case then there can be no unity where diametrically opposed interpretations of scripture have the same authority.

Temperate: No, I am not so naïve to assume that we could ever live with that arrangement. Nor am I opposed to one interpretation of scripture being the standard for church policies. I never opposed our stance on homosexuality. My question is this: Can you tolerate

---

25. For further discussion see Achtemeier, *Bible's Yes*; Myers and Scanzoni, *What God has Joined*.

a dissenting minority in our denomination? The conservative view on homosexuality is currently the rule of law in the church. If it is such an essential teaching, then why didn't we kick out the dissenters years ago? If we change our stance, why should the liberals tolerate you conservatives?

Credo: When it is simply a minority of members who err, we can tolerate them because the Holy Spirit can work through them, in spite of their mistakes, as long as they are willing to keep the covenant of our *Discipline*. When they disobey the *Discipline* then they cross the line. But as long as they respect the covenant and kept their opinions to themselves, then God can use them.

Anchor: At this point, I believe that I must stay in and continue to be a faithful witness, even if it may become an act of dissent. The only thing that will renew the United Methodist Church will be for conservatives to make a pledge to continue to uphold the prohibition on homosexual behavior.

Hound: So Anchor, the shoe may soon be on the other foot. I have heard you complain for years about liberals who were breaking Our covenant and fomenting schism because of their dissent. Aren't you suggesting that conservatives do the same thing? A covenant is a covenant, is it not? Are we not supposed to uphold the *Discipline*, regardless of what it says?

Anchor: Not if it violates Scripture. Wesley was very clear about that. Time and again he said that we are called to follow the dictates of our conscience if church law is contrary to the Bible, but he would tell us to be the loyal opposition and to let those who are wrong kick us out.[26]

Hound: So there is a place in our Wesleyan tradition for faithful dissent. Wesley was a scoundrel when it came to obeying church law. He always worked the loop holes in order to deploy his lay preachers and build his preaching houses. The overused catch

---

26. Wesley, "Catholic Spirit," 85; Wesley, "On Schism," 67.

phrase, "the world is my parish" originated as a justification for why he was violating parish boundaries. In fact, he was being criticized for promoting schism when he wrote it. What was once a great comeback line to a bishop has now become a droll slogan for church agencies.[27]

This raises a question for you liberals: How will you respond to the conservatives if and when they protest at future General Conferences just as you have done? Will you be generous and understanding when they take over the floor of a plenary session, break a chalice and put a shroud over the communion table?

Embrace: For many years, progressives have claimed that our dissent is in keeping with our Wesleyan heritage. They have been the loyal opposition. Yes, a few have crossed the line and committed "ecclesiastical disobedience" by coming out of the closet or performing gay weddings. And every time, they were punished for it.

But the majority of progressives have not crossed the line. We aired our disagreements without violating the *Discipline*. And what do they get in return? Constant criticism and harassment stirred up by those conservative caucuses who believe that they are the only ones who can judge whether someone is breaking the covenant. Our denomination has an open process for expressing our disagreements; we have a responsibility to offer constructive criticism.

Yet, every time we spoke out, the conservative caucuses ranted about how we were breaking the covenant. Every time one of our courts ruled in their favor, the conservatives hollered that the decision "strikes a blow at church unity."[28] The conservative rhetoric has been so bad that it has cut off conversation. You cannot express any disagreement with the *Discipline* without being accused of being disloyal or creating schism. A generation ago it was called "red-baiting." So what is it now, "gay-baiting"?

---

27. June 11, 1739, "Journal," 201; Baker, *John Wesley*, 63, 68.
28. *We Confess*, May/June 2005, 1.

Credo: My frustrations are not with liberals who air their disagreements through the appropriate channels. What has violated the trust of so many conservatives is the leftist fringe which has blatantly disregarded the decisions and procedures of the General Conference. For years, liberal leaders have looked down their noses at conservative pastors who worked hard and served their congregations well. They were patronizing to conservative churches—the grassroots of this denomination—assuming that their beliefs were ignorant. These leaders have no integrity when they claim the Wesleyan heritage but set out to undermine the only body that can speak for the denomination. They have no integrity when they have tried in vain to find loop holes in our polity which do not exist. They have no integrity when they control our general agencies with their leftist agenda. What we have experienced over the years is that the liberals talk about tolerance but they are unwilling to tolerate conservatives.

What Should a Bishop Do?

Anchor: How can we trust each other anymore? I am sorry if I offend any of you, but I must be honest. Some of you have brought this crisis on us because of your disregard and disobedience to the *Discipline*. You have ignored pastors who violate the *Discipline*. When charges have been filed against them, you have not ensured that the denomination's official position is defended because you allowed pastors who disagree with the *Discipline* to be the counsel for the Church. You have allowed weak sentences to be handed down against those who have been found guilty. You have stated publically that you will not uphold the *Discipline*. You have allowed the covenant of ministry to be violated and have made a mockery of the episcopal office. If anyone is to blame for the destruction of the United Methodist Church it will be some of you who are bishops with whom the unity and integrity of the church was entrusted.

Temperate: You are making some big assumptions with which I disagree. As you know, we bishops do not decide on the sentencing or the selections in the judicial process. We cannot shoulder all the blame for this mess. That is unfair. In fact, we have tried to promote unity through a common vision of ministry when we offered up the Seven Vision Pathways. We tried to create a missional unity through a new vision of a worldwide denomination.

Hound: If the General Conference delegates want to reject our efforts, then it is their fault for this mess. You can't lead a ship of fools if they are hell bent on sailing into a storm.

Leeway: I also think there is a difference between lighter sentences and completely disregarding the judicial process. A pastor may be found guilty of violating the *Discipline* but that does not mean that you have to throw the book at her. I believe in upholding the *Discipline,* but I think the punishment must fit the crime. This is where the particular pastoral context should be considered. If a gay marriage is performed in a supportive church and the event does not cause any dissension, then the punishment should be lighter because the violation caused less damage. Just because you are unhappy with a punishment does not mean that the process has been violated. I am uncomfortable with the vagueness of your accusation because it allows for anyone who disagrees to be labeled a violator. Do you recognize a distinction between disagreement and disobedience?

Credo: Disagreement in and of itself is not a violation. Clearly, disobedience is a violation. When and how the disagreement is expressed by bishops can foster violations.

As bishops, our unique role is to teach the doctrines and maintain the unity of the church. We are to "guard, transmit, teach and proclaim" the apostolic faith and "uphold the theological traditions of the United Methodist Church." In doing this we are to have "a passion for the unity of the Church. The role of the bishop is to be a shepherd for the whole flock."[29] This is what we were elected and consecrated to do.

We are not doing this when we go around expressing our own opinions that contradict the *Discipline*. We violate our task when we push the envelope by splitting hairs about compliance with the *Discipline* when we pronounce blessings and issue statements supporting gay marriage in the newspapers. To say that you are not being divisive is another form of legalism, a cynical following of the letter of the law while desecrating the spirit of it. When we do this we are not being a shepherd for the whole flock, we are being a shepherd for only one part of the flock.

Anchor: Worse, a bishop who expresses dissent is a shepherd who lets the wolf in the pasture. It is too late. You should have followed the advice of those courageous pastors who issued the statement "Integrity and Unity."[30] For those of you who want to preserve the unity of the denomination, you should have censured some of our colleagues. We should have pledged to uphold and teach the traditional view of marriage and fully enforce the *Discipline*. We should have ensured that, when counsel was appointed for the church, they were persons who fully supported the current teachings of the church.

Embrace: Both of you are making assumptions about the authority and role of a bishop that I do not share. This Council does not have the power or authority you assume it does. We are not accountable to this Council but to the jurisdictions that elected us. If there is any censuring, it should be done by the Colleges of Bishops we are a part of.

On a deeper level, you are making an assumption about how a bishop should act that I do not believe is right. You are assuming that a bishop can only uphold church unity by hiding his or her convictions. Is my opinion so powerful that the unity of church depends on my silence? That was never my understanding of the

---

29. *Discipline*, 317, 330.
30. Methodist Crossroads, "Integrity and Unity."

office. Remember, we are elders first. There is no third order of ordination. As an elder, I am not required to keep my opinion in the closet. I have a right to share my disagreement. To be sure, it must be done with sensitivity to the context and with pastoral awareness of the potential effects. But I will never agree with you that there is never a time or place for me as a bishop to express my disagreement with the *Discipline*.

Credo: But in this context, your so-called right to express your opinion is causing the ruin of our church.

Anchor: Credo and I disagree with your view of what it means to be a bishop. When I was consecrated to this task I surrendered my personal opinions at the altar so that I could lead the church in mission and unity. I do not believe that a bishop should express his or her opinion. Perhaps this is the difference between the role of an elder as a pastor and the role of an elder as a bishop. Our role is to be a spokesperson and representative of the church, and our standing in the denomination is too prominent and complex to be able to step out of that role in order to express one's personal opinion.

Temperate: I thought the unity of the church was a gift from God. God has always protected the church from incompetent leaders, and if you are right, then I trust in God to protect us from ourselves.

Is Schism a Sin?

Anchor: I trust God to give us the opportunity to remain united, but we also have the free will to reject that gift. In 1844 what tipped the scales for separation was a controversy surrounding a bishop who owned a slave. Perhaps the same is happening now because of what some of you have done or failed to do. I believe our schism occurred years ago, and tonight we are only waiting to see whether it culminates in separation. Wesley's description of schism is poignant. In his sermon "On Schism" he said that it is the lack of "tender care for each other . . . an alienation of affection . . . a division of heart" that occurs within the church even though we are still outwardly united.[31] Separation is the logical outcome of the sin of schism gone unchecked.

Temperate: Just because we have schism does not mean that we should pursue separation. We have sinned against each other in the way we have handled our differences but separating would only increase our sins. I know it sounds tempting. But Wesley knew a thing or two about this temptation. When schism metastasizes into separation "it brings forth evil fruit . . . It opens a door to all unkind tempers, both in ourselves and others. It leads directly to a whole train of evil surmisings, to severe and uncharitable judging of each other . . . creating a present hell . . . as a prelude to hell eternal."[32] Am I hitting close to home?

On a personal level, it creates a church culture in which it is difficult to cultivate the habits and attitudes that help each of us grow in grace. On a missional level, it becomes a stumbling block for non-believers who see us as yet another example of Protestants splintering over the latest controversial issue.[33]

What bothers me most is the way this one issue obscures all of the other problems and sins that are preventing us from being a faithful church. For the typical United Methodist congregation, the real schism is between the trustees and the education committee over who is in charge of the education wing. The greater impediment to evangelism is our apathy, not immorality.

Tonight's conversation is out of touch with the reality of the local church, and the General Conference has been out of touch with the local church. It is never clean and pure at the local level. Our members and churches are a mixed breed of opinions, often inconsistent and inarticulate. It is only in the reified air of General Conference that the ideologies sort themselves out so neatly into political caucuses. If we were truly led by the realities of the local

---

31. Wesley, "On Schism," 63.
32. Ibid., 65.
33. Ibid., 66.

church, this entire conversation would sound and feel different. That does not mean we would agree. Hardly, but I suspect that separation would not be a serious option. Because at the local level, people have learned to work around each other's sins for years, and our healthy local churches know how to work through their disagreements.

Credo: You speak of unity within a local church, but this is an issue of unity among congregations. How can connectionalism be meaningful if we cannot express our unity on a fundamental issue such as this?

Temperate: I disagree with your assumption that this is a fundamental issue. It raises fundamental issues, to be sure, but it has been given too much importance. There is a problem when a single contemporary issue is elevated to such importance that the unity of the church stands or falls on it. Therefore, both sides are wrong. Progressives are wrong for using disobedience to express their disagreements with the *Discipline*. Conservatives are wrong to suggest that any changes to the *Discipline* are unacceptable.

Hound: The truth be told, we could draft a plan for separation tomorrow and it would not make one wit of difference to our local churches. It would not bring about their renewal because real renewal means changing the culture of the denomination, No amount of tinkering with or even overhauling the *Discipline* will accomplish that feat. So, you liberals, go ahead and ordain homosexuals and write liturgies to bless their relationships. Our congregations will find other ways to keep them out of the pulpit, and they will ignore any revisions to the *Book of Worship.* And go ahead, you conservatives, and pass as many prohibitions against them as you want. Any local church that wants to welcome them into their fellowship will keep on ignoring the *Discipline.* In the end, the issue of homosexuality will be like the issue of contraceptives in the Roman Catholic Church: a deeply entrenched social teaching that very few laypersons believe in or practice.

Temperate: All I am saying is that if you want to be effective, if you want to enact real change it has to come from the bottom up. If you want to find God's renewal in this controversy, it means listening closely and keeping connected with the local church. I know there is the danger in parochialism in what I am saying. Notice, that I did not say "your" local church because then we will only be listening to people like ourselves. We must stay connected with the diversity of local churches across the connectionalism.

Let me take the boldly moderate proposition that we are stuck with each other for good reason. I am not saying that we should settle for a mushy middle where we don't take a controversial stance. I believe God wants us to stay together so that each of us can grow in grace. This is one of the common themes I see in healthy and growing local churches. Our disagreements and controversies are opportunities to push us on toward Christian perfection.

It is in the way we handle our differences that the fruit of the Spirit is cultivated. It is in being patient with our brothers and sisters who are in error that we learn to entrust the church to God's protection. It is in having our brothers and sisters point out our errors that we learn to be humble. If you let schism lead to separation you lose out on this opportunity to grow, as individuals and as a denomination.

Hound: But let's face it, the only things that are really holding us together are our pension fund and our property, not our desire to move on toward Christian perfection.

Temperate: So what if it is! So what if the main thing that is keeping us together is the bureaucracy. Don't you think that the Holy Spirit can use even a moribund bureaucracy to bring about our salvation? The wind blows where it will. Maybe God is forcing us to stay together through these crass means until we mature enough so that our faith in God's grace is what fully unites us.

In order to keep receiving that gift we have to keep talking to each other and stay committed to one another. Many complain that we have rehashed the issue of homosexuality for the past forty

Part Two

years and everyone is tired of talking about it. I would suggest that the conversation has barely begun. We have talked at each other and past each other; we have used it for political gain and we have done a lot of posturing and belly aching. But the conversation has been shallow and shrill. We have not explored the deeper issues of doctrine and authority, discipline and interpretation because our connectionalism is weak. But the conversation is worth it because it has the potential to make each of us more holy and to deepen our understanding of the faith.

Compass: Unity is a strange gift from God. For those of you who believe that the denomination should remain intact, this process will make us stronger and more united. For those of you who think that separation is inevitable and desirable, then you need this conversation to prepare you for that day. But I do not think that day has come. We are not ready for it.

The Spirit cannot move our conversation to a deeper level unless we have a humble and repentant heart. That is the prerequisite to any grace-filled conversation. That does not mean that you must abandon your position, but it does mean that you defend it while at the same time you abandon your life. This means that liberals must stop using rituals and general church meetings as political theater. This means that conservatives must stop crying wolf about schism and violations of a covenant. Regardless of what happens tomorrow, we can all agree on one point that Wesley demands of us: "Then if we cannot as yet *think alike* in all things, at least we may *love alike*. Herein we cannot possibly do amiss."[34] I am convinced that what is most important may not be what we decide but how we decide it. We must love one another for God is love. Let us pray together:

All: "Help each of us, gracious God, to live in such magnanimity and restraint that the Head of the church may never have cause to say to any of us, 'This is my body, broken by you.' Amen."[35]

---

34. Wesley, "Letter to a Roman Catholic," 498.
35. *Hymnal*, 564.

Bibliography

Abraham, William J. "Ecumenism and the Rocky Road to Renewal." In *The Ecumenical Future*. Edited by Carl E. Braaten and Robert W. Jenson, 176–187. Grand Rapids: Eerdmans, 2004.

Achtemeier, Mark. *The Bible's Yes to Same-Sex Marriage: An Evangelical's Change of Heart*. Louisville: Westminster John Knox, 2014.

Baker, Frank. *John Wesley and the Church of England*. Nashville: Abingdon Press, 1970.

Best, Gary. *Charles Wesley*. Peterborough: Epworth, 2006.

Bonhoeffer, Dietrich. *The Cost of Discipleship*. New York: Touchstone, 1995.

The Book of Discipline of the United Methodist Church. Nashville: United Methodist Publishing House, 2012.

Case, Riley B. "An Historic Review of Local Pastor Authority Regarding Membership." *We Confess* 11, no. 6, Nov/Dec 2005, 4–5.

Collins, Kenneth. *The Scripture Way of Salvation*. Nashville: Abingdon, 1997.

The Council of Bishops. "A Pastoral Letter to the People of The United Methodist Church from the Council of Bishops," Lake Junaluska, November 2, 2005.

Furnish, Victor Paul. "The Bible and Homosexuality: Reading the Texts in Context." In *Homosexuality in the Church*. Edited by Jeffrey S. Siker, 18–38. Louisville: Westminster John Knox, 1994.

Hays, Richard B. *The Moral Vision of the New Testament*, New York: HarperCollins, 1996.

Heitzenrater, Richard P. *Wesley and the People Called Methodists*. Nashville: Abingdon, 1995.

Judicial Council. *Decision* 1032. (October, 28, 2005) http://www.umc.org/decisions/41942/eyJy zxn1bhrfcgfnzsi6ilwvzgvjaxnpb 25zxc9zzwfyy2gtcmvzdwx0cyisinnlyxjjadpkzwnpc2lvbl90exblijoimsj9

Methodist Crossroads. "Integrity and Unity." Accessed May 13, 2015, www.methodistcrossroads.org/?p=1.

Morse, Christopher. *Not Every Spirit: A Dogmatics of Christian Disbelief*. Valley Forge: Trinity, 1994.

Myers, David G. and Letha Dawson Scanzoni, *What God has Joined Together: the Christian Case for Gay Marriage,* New York: Harper-Collins, 2005.

Bibliography

Resolution 8032. "This Holy Mystery: A United Methodist Understanding of Holy Communion." In *The Book of Resolutions of the United Methodist Church* 2012, 942-91. Nashville: United Methodist Publishing House, 2012.

Ruth, Lester. *A Little Heaven Below*. Nashville: Kingswood, 2000.

Scroggs, Robin. *The New Testament and Homosexuality*. Minneapolis: Fortress, 1983.

The United Methodist Hymnal: Book of United Methodist Worship. Nashville: United Methodist Publishing House, 1989.

"United Methodism's Vows at Risk." *Good News*, March/April 2006, 9.

"Unity In Christ, That the World May Believe." *We Confess*, vol. 11, Issue 5, Sept/Oct 2005, p. 3.

"A Way Forward," accessed November 21, 2014, http://awayforward.net/.

Wesley, John. "On Attending the Church Service." In vol. 3, *The Works of John Wesley*. Edited by Albert C. Outler, 465-78. Nashville: Abingdon, 1986.

———. "On Baptism." In *John Wesley*. Edited by Albert C. Outler, 318-32. Oxford: Oxford University Press, 1964.

———. "Catholic Spirit." In vol.2. The Works of John Wesley. Edited by Albert C. Outler, 81-95. Nashville: Abingdon, 1985.

———. "A Caution Against Bigotry." In vol. 2, *The Works of John Wesley*. Edited by Albert C. Outler, 63-78. Nashville: Abingdon, 1985.

———. "Of the Church." In vol. 3, *The Works of John Wesley*. Edited by Albert C. Outler, 46-57. Nashville: Abingdon, 1986.

———. "The Duty of Constant Communion." In vol. 3, *The Works of John Wesley*. Edited by Albert C. Outler, 428-39. Nashville: Abingdon, 1986.

———."An Earnest Appeal to Men of Reason and Religion." In *John Wesley*. Edited by Albert C. Outler, 385-424. Oxford: Oxford University Press, 1964.

———. *Explanatory Notes Upon the New Testament*. 2 volumes. Grand Rapids: Baker, 1986.

———."Farther Thoughts on Separation from the Church." In vol. 9, *The Works of John Wesley*. Edited by Rupert E. Davies, 538-40. Nashville: Abingdon, 1989.

———. "The First Annual Conference." In *John Wesley*. Edited by Albert C. Outler, 136-47. New York: Oxford University Press, 1964.

———. "On God's Vineyard." In vol. 3, *The Works of John Wesley*. Edited by Albert C. Outler, 503-17. Nashville: Abingdon, 1986.

———. Journal from October 14, 1735 to November 29, 1745. Vol. 1, *The Works of John Wesley*. Grand Rapids: Zondervan.

———. "Letter to a Roman Catholic." In *John Wesley*. Edited by Albert C. Outler, 493-9. Oxford: Oxford University Press, 1964.

———. "The Means of Grace." In vol. 1, *The Works of John Wesley*. Edited by Albert C. Outler, 378-97. Nashville: Abingdon, 1984.

———. "The Mystery of Iniquity." In vol. 2, *The Works of John Wesley*. Edited by Albert C. Outler, 452-470. Nashville: Abingdon, 1985.

Bibliography

———. "The Nature, Design, and General Rules of the United Societies." In vol. 9, *In The Works of John Wesley*. Edited by Rupert E. Davies, 69–73. Nashville: Abingdon, 1989.

———. "Ought We to Separate from the Church of England?" In *John Wesley and the Church of England*. Frank Baker, 326-340. Nashville: Abingdon, 1970.

———. "The Principles of a Methodist." In vol. 9, *In The Works of John Wesley*. Edited by Rupert E. Davies, 48–66. Nashville: Abingdon, 1989.

———. "The Principles of a Methodist Farther Explained." In vol. 9, *In The Works of John Wesley*. Edited by Rupert E. Davies, 161–237. Nashville: Abingdon, 1989.

———. "Prophets and Priests." In vol. 4, *The Works of John Wesley*. Edited by Albert C. Outler, 75–84. Nashville: Abingdon, 1987.

———. "The Real Character of Montanus." In vol. 11, *The Works of John Wesley*, 485–486. Grand Rapids: Zondervan, 1872.

———. "Reasons Against a Separation from the Church of England." In vol. 9, *In The Works of John Wesley*. Edited by Rupert E. Davies, 334–49. Nashville: Abingdon, 1989.

———. "The Reformation of Manners." In vol. 2, *The Works of John Wesley*. Edited by Albert C. Outler, 301–23. Nashville: Abingdon, 1985.

———. "On Schism." In vol. 3, *The Works of John Wesley*. Edited by Albert C. Outler, 59–69. Nashville: Abingdon, 1986.

———. "Thoughts Upon Methodism." In vol. 9, *The Works of John Wesley*. Edited by Rupert E. Davies, 527–30. Nashville: Abingdon, 1987.

———. "The Unity of the Divine Being." In vol. 3, *The Works of John Wesley*. Edited by Albert C. Outler, 61–71. Nashville: Abingdon, 1987.

———. "The Way of the Kingdom." In vol. 1, *The Works of John Wesley*. Edited by Albert C. Outler, 218–232. Nashville: Abingdon, 1984.

Williams, Colin W. *John Wesley's Theology Today*. Nashville: Abingdon, 1960.